FAMILY Style

FAMILY Style

INTERIOR DESIGN
WITH CHILDREN IN MIND
gardens too

JUDITH ROBERTSON

**DRAGON'S
WORLD**

FOR GRAEME,
LUCY AND LIBBY

This book has taken several years of gleaning ideas and thoughts from my family and friends – I would like to thank them all for the part they have played.

Grateful thanks are due to my editor Nicky Adamson who added all her invaluable expertise in publishing and parenting, and turned my 'stream of consciousness' into an organized readable book with commas.

I would also like to thank Piers Bizony and Richard Vanspall of Longroom Studio for all the hard work and thought they put into the photographs, Caroline and John Astrop for their lovely illustrations, Hilary Davies for the detailed architectural drawings, Pippa Rubinstein for her encouragement and seeing the potential in the original idea, Sheila Buff for her input from across the Atlantic and Maureen Hegarty, Diana Steedman, Keith Bambury at Dragon's World for their hard work and cheery backup.

Dragon's World Ltd
Limpsfield
Surrey RH8 0DY
Great Britain

First published by Dragon's World 1990

© Dragon's World 1990
© Text Judith Robertson 1990
© Special photography Piers Bizony and Richard Vanspall of Longroom Studio 1990

Design and Art Direction   **Judith Robertson**
Editor   **Nicky Adamson**
Editorial Director   **Pippa Rubinstein**

British Library Cataloguing in Publication Data

Robertson, Judith
  Family style: interior design with children in mind.
  1. Residences. Interior design
  I. Title
  747

ISBN 1 85028 103 3

Typeset by Bookworm Typesetting, Manchester
Printed in Singapore

CONTENTS

LOOKING AT YOUR HOME

LEFT This lovely conservatory leads from the kitchen to the garden. The blinds attached to the glass roof ensure that it doesn't get too hot, but do not obscure any light, leaving no excuse to avoid violin practice. In a sunny position this conservatory is as much for enjoying the sun as for growing plants.

The aim of this book is to help you escape from the idea that good design and children don't mix – on the contrary the definition of good design is that it works, so it follows that a well-designed home that takes children's needs into consideration will be much easier to maintain. If you can provide your children with a safe, comfortable environment, then you as parents can be more relaxed and able to enjoy them.

Interior design is very personal; the way rooms and houses are decorated and furnished is a matter of individual – adult – expression. Modern concepts of interior design do often clash with the needs and preoccupations of a growing family. But it needn't be like this. With forward planning, you can create an attractive and practical environment which takes the needs of all family members into account and can survive the rigours of children's use and abuse.

Whether you are planning a family and need to think about fitting an extra person into your existing home, or whether you are moving to a larger house because the size of your family is increasing, or whether you are simply taking a long hard look at a home in which children are already in residence, there will be many decisions to be made about design and safety in order to prevent future problems from occurring. It is unfortunately a fact of life that what works well for adults living without children, may not do so well for a household with them.

When you start to look at your home with children in mind, it is worth thinking about your family's changing needs over the period you expect to be living there. When they are

ABOVE On a hot summer's day, there's nothing like standing under a sprinkler in your clothes with a few interesting friends.

young, you need to be as close to them as possible, providing open areas where you can easily see what's going on. When they become teenagers, however, everything changes and they may spend a lot of time closeted in their rooms – they themselves may have more or less reached their adult size and your home may suddenly feel rather small for you all. Yet it will only be another few years before they are young adults, only coming home to do their washing. This means that you might need to think about moving to a larger home earlier than you imagined, or you may find yourself spending time and money on a larger house that your children are busy moving out of.

No two families are alike and homes come in different shapes and sizes. Each family has its own special needs and interests and economic constraints which will modify their requirements of a home. In addition, what parents are prepared to tolerate from their children can vary enormously. For instance, some like to separate their children's activities from more 'adult' areas of the home; others are happy to share most or all the living space with their children. Others don't have the space and therefore the choice to make these distinctions. A wide variety of situations are taken into account in this book to ensure that there are good ideas to suit everyone.

Children's natural exuberance and experimentation are rarely taken into account in the design of buildings and furniture, so that a child's natural use of them can frequently be misinterpreted as abuse. It is not because they are inherently bad or destructive but because they have to fit in with what is already in place in the home and need to be taught what is acceptable and safe behaviour and what is not. It helps not to lose sight of how much fun can be had in a room containing nothing but a pile of old mattresses or a large cardboard box, even if that is not how we ourselves would choose to furnish our homes!

As your children's social life develops so does the wear and tear on your home. There will be increasing numbers of visiting children who will become your responsibility while they are with you, and although your own children will know what is or isn't allowed, you will have peace of mind if you know your home is as safe and indestructible as possible

PRACTICAL CONSIDERATIONS

There are many aspects of interior design which adults take for granted, but which need to be given a bit more thought when there are children in the home. The advice in this section is partly to protect your furnishings and possessions from your children, but equally to protect your children from the possibility of accidents. Each chapter of the book gives specific advice on safety where relevant – what follows is more general and applies all over the home.

Many of the photographs in interior design books and magazines can make the average parent feel completely inadequate – whose house looks a mess, no matter how hard you try. Alternatively you may find yourself permanently on edge, ready to pounce on the children if they so much as look at a pot of powder paint near a carpet. How do people manage to live without anyone so much as squashing the cushions, let alone chipping the paint? The truth is, most people don't.

This spacious family room on two levels is an ideal space in which to perform a play, kitted out in the entire contents of the dressing up basket, while checking on how good you look in the mirror, before a captive audience in the kitchen. The room was redesigned in this way when the children of the family were over the age of five, when the introduction of a floor-to-ceiling mirror and steps were no longer a hazard to the children. The kitchen is only a small element of the room, which has the dining room leading off it to the right, so with the sofa and television in here the children hardly ever use the living room that adjoins the kitchen on the other side.

The kitchen table acts mainly as a work surface, only being used for meals for two or three people, as the dining room is so convenient. (The dining room is featured on p 57.)

CHILDREN'S AGES

Children grow and develop at very different rates, but for the purposes of this book I have defined age-groups as follows:

Babies – Birth to one year
Very young children – One to three years
Young children – Four to six years
Older children – Seven to eleven years
Young teenagers – Twelve to fourteen years
Older teenagers – Fifteen to nineteen years

This large room is almost always sunny because it has windows on three sides of it. It is a kitchen, a living room and a dining room, with a playroom leading off it. Working on the principal that while the children are young they are going to be playing wherever their parents are, the playroom was deliberately designed not to be a large room to maximize the space in the rest of the room. Although it is easily big enough to play in, the toys are often brought into the living area, but they can be swept away and stored in the playroom with the door firmly shut on them. The floor is covered with cork tiles that will be replaced when the children are older. The sofa is covered with a machine washable loose cover.

It takes time, sometime hours, to prepare a real kitchen for photography. All the old plastic carrier bags and unopened junk mail will have been tidied away; there will probably be strategically placed vases of fresh flowers, and every last teaspoon will have been carefully arranged if it is in shot.

This may seem like cheating, but who wants to see someone else's dirty plates? If you are honest with yourself, you would tidy up if someone was taking a picture of your kitchen. It's a bit like combing your hair before a family photograph. It's unrealistic, impossible and probably unhealthy to expect a home with children in it to be immaculate all the time, but you can make it quick and easy to clear up and keep clean.

TELEPHONES

Wall-mounted telephones are better than table top ones, while the children are young. There is an inevitable fascination with telephones which often leads to the phone being left off the hook. The best height for the phone is 5ft (150cm) off the floor so that a child who is old enough to answer the telephone sensibly can reach it and an adult doesn't have to bend down to dial. Make sure that the cord doesn't dangle too far down. Find an old telephone that your small child can play with instead.

If the parents of teenage children are to be believed, all teenagers think that money grows on trees, especially where telephone bills are concerned. There are telephones especially designed to deal with the problem, so you will need to investigate to find the right one that suits your household.

FLOORS

In a family home floors have to be resilient, not show the dirt and be easy to clean. It makes sense to avoid light-coloured flooring near any outside door or in a bathroom where the floor gets wet.

CARPETS When you are buying carpet talk to the retailer about whether it should be sprayed with a stain retarder or whether it has one built in. Try to train your children to let you know at once when they have spilt anything on the carpet. Spills are by definition accidents, so promise them you will not be angry if they come to you straight away, and stick to your side of the bargain. Then, if spills happen, soak up as much excess liquid as you can before turning to the stain removal chart on page 168.

FLOOR RUGS If you lay rugs over smooth flooring like stripped floorboards or vinyl, the rugs must have an efficient underfelt that stops them from sliding or moving at all. Easily the best one, called 'Fulda Carpet Stop', looks like a giant washing up sponge (see addresses on p. 172). Even rugs that are on fitted carpets can ruck up dangerously and the underlay should be used here as well.

SQUEAKING FLOORBOARDS AND STAIRS If you have ever paced up and down with a small baby in the middle of the night, you will know every squeaking floorboard, especially the one just outside the baby's room which lets out the loudest squeak just as you've got your precious bundle off to sleep.

If you suffer from this problem, which is particularly prevalent in an older house after central heating has been installed, lift the carpet and make sure all the floorboards are nailed down securely. There are a few different ways to get rid of these squeaks, and it can depend where they are as to how you treat them. Consult a DIY manual. If you are about to have carpets fitted deal with the squeaks first.

DECORATION

When your children are very young, doing the decorating is a real struggle and if you can afford it it is worth hiring a decorator to do it for you. Otherwise the children have to be taken out or they end up covered in paint.

Paintwork on doors and skirting (base) boards needs to be very carefully prepared to stand up to the knocks they will receive. Gloss paint always chips eventually, no matter what you do with it. If there is already paint on your skirting boards and it is quite old and brittle you may need to strip them down to the wood, then prime, undercoat and gloss paint them again. This will cut down the chipping but unfortunately, a completely chip-proof paint has yet to be developed. Skirting boards stripped and waxed or varnished with a couple of layers of polyurethane hide the scuffs well and any chips out of the finish don't show so easily.

Choosing colours from paint charts and wallpaper books isn't easy for most people, the samples are usually extremely small and you don't know whether you like the colour until you've pratically finished the room. So wherever possible buy a roll of paper and pin it up or buy a few small pots of

The wallpaper and matching border give this bedroom a light, fresh look and because the paper is washable it will last until the occupant needs a new look to match her teenage maturity.

paint to look at the colour in situ. If you have time to live with it for a few days, it helps to give you more of an idea of what the finished decoration will look like.

The finish on the walls must be as durable and washable as possible throughout your home – children get everywhere. Vinyl silk (latex semigloss) and matt paints are washable and come in a full range of colours.

Interesting paint effects, such as sponging and marbling, conceal fingerprints and are easy to apply. Wallpapers should be washable. Vinyl wallpapers do wash, but they peel away from their backing very easily to make repapering easier. This is a breakthrough for the DIY market, but if your children are still at the 'if it peels, pull it' stage, you may find that they have a lovely quiet ten minutes picking the paper off the wall somewhere rather noticeable.

As yet there is nothing on the market that doesn't mark the wall that can be used for hanging posters and pictures. Pin holes probably show the least, so the answer is to use bulletin boards, wherever possible.

SOUNDPROOFING

Soundproofing is not a simple matter of putting a blanket between the piano and the wall to deaden the sound, or closing the door to keep the sound of the hifi in. This really doesn't work well enough. Real soundproofing is a major undertaking. It requires a floating floor, 7in (17.5cm) above the original floor, a suspended or independent ceiling 3 ¾in (9.5cm) below the original ceiling, and separating walls, with a soundproofing quilt between them and the original walls, with a loss of 6in (15cm) of space for each wall. It may be cheaper and easier to send her to the garage or basement if your child is going to take up the drums.

PREVENTING ACCIDENTS

There are two kinds of safety precautions where children are involved – those that we put into effect because they directly affect the person who is looking after the child, and the other kind that we always mean to do and may not get round to. An example of the first is a stair gate which stops a very young child from crawling up the stairs with the apparent intention of falling down them, so that you have to stop whatever you are doing to go and pick him up and carry him down to safety, only to allow him to do it again in ten seconds time. Sometimes you can be patient and encourage these investigative instincts, but more often than not you haven't got the time, so you go and buy a stair gate. An example of the second is the lack of childproofing on the cupboard under the kitchen sink where all the dangerous cleaners are kept, or the medicines kept just out of reach in the bathroom, but readily accessible to the agile toddler. This is the 'It'll never happen to me' syndrome. It might take a severe fright to get you to make the necessary preventive measures – such as finding your child about to eat the dishwashing powder.

You can avoid both the above scenarios of course by doing something about safety precautions *before* either irritation or fear drive you to it. Safety in the home is most definitely a matter of attitude – of thinking ahead to cover as many eventualities as possible and not just assuming that it will not

The vibrant blues and purples in this kitchen might be considered brave but they make the space interesting and all the surfaces are easy to keep clean. Plentiful cupboards and shelves mean that the counters are not cluttered with kitchen equipment, and simple details like the window painted in pink are echoed in the open plan living room that is beyond the divider at the rear. Any food preparation is hidden from the living room but the cook can be part of any conversation or keep an eye on a small child playing in there.
The narrow slatted venetian blinds provide a clean line that lets light in but with slight adjustment can give as much privacy as needed. The floor is covered with nonslip vinyl sheeting.

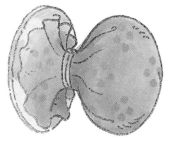

One simple and effective DIY method to prevent small children entering rooms where they are not allowed, is to place a 7½in (180mm) diameter circle of fabric over the door knob, secured with an elastic band. (All door knobs should be properly fitted to make sure a child doesn't get shut in a room, which can be very frightening.)

happen to you. Hospitals are full of people who thought it would never happen to them. And even if you have done everything that you can think of to childproof your home, things can happen which are unfortunately impossible to predict, so you have to be on your guard, especially while your children are under five years old.

CHILDPROOF PRODUCTS Childproof products are strictly speaking child-*resistant* rather than *proof*, but almost all of them can be useful to you at some time. Aspects of safety are dealt with throughout the chapters in this book, but you will need to think about where your own specific problem areas are, and deal with them before they become a hazard.

These small, unobtrusive brackets can make a free-standing bookcase safe from falling on a child who thinks there just might be some sweets hidden on the top shelf.

PLUGS, SOCKETS AND WIRES Although it is not easy for children to poke things into modern electric sockets, with very young children in the house it is wise always to cover them to make sure that no child can push something in and give himself an electric shock. These covers are cheap to buy and easy to use. There are childproof plugs and sockets on the market that you push in and turn, which make it impossible for even the most inquisitive child to hurt himself (see addresses on p. 172).

Wires must never dangle or trail, no matter what age your children are. Coiled cables, similar to telephone cables, are very useful for electrical equipment.

WINDOW LOCKS You may have thought of window locks simply in terms of keeping intruders out, but they are also extremely important for any window above the ground floor to keep your children in, especially while they are very young.

For sash windows security bolts that only allow the window to be opened 5in (130mm) from the bottom are effective. Skylight windows in the roof can be fitted with a safety lock which only allows them to be opened a little way. If you want to be able to open them wide fit vertical wooden bars across the bottom half of the window, on the inside. This is particularly important if the windows are quite low down. Any window that opens outwards must have a lock on it that only allows it to open 5in (130mm). (See p. 73 for a perspex window guard.) If you haven't got safety locks on your windows yet make it a habit that only the top part of a sash window is ever opened and that nothing is kept under a window to climb up on. In some parts of America window gates are required by law for apartments where there are young children. Check with your building management.

Window locks must be designed for use with the specific style of window that you have. This one, for casement windows, prevents the window from being opened more than about 5in (12.5cm). Some but not all safety locks double as security locks.

FIRE SAFETY

Because a fire spreads very quickly, and at night it's not usually discovered until later than it would be in the daytime, it's worth preparing your family for a fast exit, if there is ever the need for it. Make sure the whole family knows the rule:

GET OUT; CALL THE FIRE SERVICE; STAY OUT.

Plan your escape routes and practice them every so often. If at all possible there should be two escape routes from every room. If your windows have window locks, put the key on a hook where children over six can reach it, (see reach chart p. 169), and show them how to use it, making it clear that

This type of adjustable and movable stair gate is much easier and safer for an adult to use than the type you have to climb over. You may need to have two stair gates, one at the top and one at the bottom of the stairs, so they need to be easy for the rest of the family to use.

this is strictly for emergencies only. If you fit double glazing, make sure at least one window in each room is easy to open, as the glass is almost impossible to break.

If you do discover a fire in your home, get everyone out of the room where the fire has started and close the door, then get them to safety as quickly as possible, without panicking them. Ensure everyone is out of the house, but leave everything else and call the fire brigade. Do not attempt to re-enter the house.

As most fires happen at night, close all doors at bedtime. Look for low flammability labels when buying night clothes for your children. Foam-filled furniture should only be 'combustion-modified' – look for the green label, or the words 'combustion-modified' on the label, when buying new furniture – which means that it won't ignite if a lighted match is dropped on it and is resistant to cigarettes. The older type of foam ignites in minutes and gives off highly toxic fumes.

SMOKE ALARMS You will probably need more than one smoke alarm, but the most important place for a smoke alarm is on the ceiling in the hall at the bottom of the stairs between the sleeping area and the most likely source of the fire – the living room or kitchen. It needs to be placed on the ceiling because smoke rises to the highest point and billows across the ceiling. Preferably there should be a smoke alarm in the hall, the living room, outside the bedrooms on the landings and in the bedrooms.

It is best to change the batteries of smoke alarms once a year. Make sure the alarms are loud enough for the family to hear them and be woken by them. It is worth testing them when the children are asleep to see whether they wake up. Reassure them the moment they wake up that you are just testing the alarm, but explain that next time might be the real thing.

FIRE EXTINGUISHERS There should be an extinguisher next to each exterior door of your home and a fire blanket for chip pan fires in the kitchen (see p. 32). Extinguishers should be out of reach of children under the age of twelve, and you need to explain when and how to use them. Read the instructions carefully every so often as you are passing the extinguisher so that you know exactly what to do if you ever need to use it.

FAMILY FIRE DRILL When your children are six or over it is a good idea to discuss with them what to do in case of a fire, without frightening them. Show them a couple of routes to leave by. Point out that fire spreads quickly and that there is a lot of smoke, so they have to act quickly and it may be dark. Get them to play a sort of game whereby they have to get to the front or back door from their bedroom, blindfolded (to simulate darkness and thick smoke), and on their hands and knees, (because smoke rises, the breathable air is left nearest the floor). Watch them carefully to make sure they don't hurt themselves as they go.

If escaping out of a first floor window is likely to be an option, explain to children that they should try to throw out as many things as possible first that are soft to land on, like duvets, blankets and pillows, or best of all, mattresses, although these are very heavy and difficult to move.

ESCAPE DRILL CHECKLIST

"Get everyone to remember the following drill if cut off by fire.

Close the door and any other openings and block the cracks with bedding etc.

Go to the window, try to attract attention and wait for the fire brigade.

If the room becomes smokey stay low.
It is easier to breathe. Think about making your escape.

If the window is jammed, break it.
Remove jagged glass from the lower sill and cover it with a blanket.

Drop cushions or bedding to the ground to break your fall.

Get out feet first and lower yourself to the full length of your arms before dropping.

Avoid jumping unless forced to.
Unnecessary injury often occurs in this way".

SMOKE ALARM BATTERIES

It is recommended that batteries are changed once a year, choose a birthday of one member of the family and make that the day you always change the battery.

HALLS, STAIRS & LANDINGS

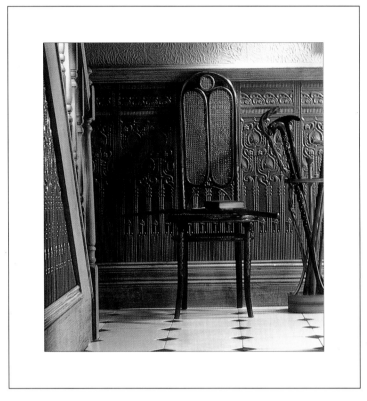

ABOVE *The textured*
wallpaper below the dado rail in
this entrance hall has been
painted with gloss paint for easy
cleaning in a colour that will
hide any finger marks. All the
wood surfaces – skirting (base)
boards, dado rail and bannisters
– have been treated with a paint
technique called dragging, in a
slightly lighter colour, and the
upper part of the walls and the
flooring are light to offset the
darker areas. In this particular
hall, stairs lead up directly from
the front door, so that any mud
brought in would have been left
on the large coconut mat just
inside it.

In many homes the entrance hall or lobby is a dead area, but with careful thought, it could provide extra storage or playing space, or even the equivalent of an extra room. Instead, it is all too often used as a dumping ground for bikes, bags, junk mail, ladders, baby paraphernalia and so on.

Halls come in as many different shapes and sizes as there are of houses and apartments. If yours is particularly large or long, it could be an ideal play area for small children, who need lots of space within earshot of the person who is looking after them. The corridors of an apartment on one level make a perfect place to ride a small tricycle up and down.

DECORATION

WALL TREATMENTS Walls in the hall, staircase and landing need to be protected from the onslaught of grubby hands running along them, bikes being ridden into them and parked against them, so the underlying plaster should be sound, and the decorative covering must be durable and washable. Vinyl silk emulsion (latex semigloss) is a good finish for a hall and stairway, with at least three layers of gloss or enamel paint, or polyurethane varnish, on the skirting (base) boards and balustrade to withstand knocks (see p.11 for the best preparation).

When you are choosing colours for your hall remember that the light changes from one area to another, especially if it leads to a staircase, and the colour is usually continued

RIGHT *Baskets hung simply*
from nails on the wall solve the
problem of how to store them
and provide interesting and
varied decoration in this wide
entrance hall. They also provide
handy storage for the various
seasonal small items that tend to
get left by the front door – like
scarves and gloves, the dog's
lead, tennis balls and baseball
mitts. The baskets themselves
may be pressed into use from
time to time so the display is
always changing. Another
basket on the table holds
cameras and letters safely until
claimed by their rightful owners.
In this hall the space under the
stairs has been opened up to
provide more room and a toilet
has been fitted in as well. A long
shelf holds sports equipment like
tennis rackets. The loud hailer is
essential in this household, to
call the children in for supper, so
that any adults have a voice left
for conversation at the table.

This narrow hall uses tongue and groove slats of wood below a higher than average dado rail, painted with gloss paint. The cool grey-blue which reflects as much light as possible from the glass door panels is offset by the warmth of stripped and varnished floorboards. A coat and shoe cupboard tucked under the stairs just inside the door prevents any unnecessary clutter.

throughout hall and stairwell. You may need to experiment with the darkest and lightest areas first to see whether the colour you have chosen works in both.

The old-fashioned idea of a dado rail works very well in a family home because it helps to hide fingerprints and knocks on the lower half of the wall. This late Victorian decorative feature, consisting of a thin bevelled wooden rail pinned and glued to the wall about three feet or one metre above the floor, was often combined with a painted, textured anaglypta paper between skirting board and dado, with smooth walls above in a contrasting colour or paper. Suitable moulded strips are readily available in DIY stores.

Painted vertical tongue and groove boards below the dado rail could be a charming alternative to anaglypta, giving a slightly rustic look. Either way, the traditional idea of having a darker colour in a gloss or other washable paint below the dado is sensible since this is the area which is most vulnerable to marks in a family home. The wall above can be any finish you like, including wallpaper, in a lighter tone.

A hand-rail up the wall side of the stairs also helps to avoid fingerprints from small children who tend to use the wall for support when they first begin to negotiate the stairs on two feet instead of all fours. If your stairs are narrow and a rail would protrude too far, a thick rope run as taut as possible through rings looks interesting and does not reduce the width. Alternatively you could consider a stencilled design going up the stairs at hand height to hide a lot of marks and create a very individual and attractive look, providing much needed continuity from hall to stairway. Stencilling is quite simple with the many commercial stencils now available.

PICTURES Local maps pasted onto the wall or hung near the front door look wonderful and can be useful. The hall is a good place to put up some of the better children's pictures in a simple clip frame (see p. 35). In the same way family snaps can be mounted and framed and changed frequently, rather than being left in their packets or an album, only to be looked at occasionally.

The wall up a staircase is a large area which can be covered with pictures. If you are intending to hang a sequence of prints, it is worth planning to make sure they work equally well when looked at going up and down. Much more interesting is a huge random gallery of lots of different pictures covering as much of the wall as possible – old pictures and prints from junk shops interspersed with that enormous canvas that your nephew thrust on you after his art school diploma show, beautiful examples of geometry painstakingly drawn out by your own children, clip-framed cuttings from newspapers and magazines, book-jackets or comic covers, your children's music certificates – in fact anything that is interesting and nicely but simply framed covering as much of the wall as possible. And yet another idea is to hang one big textile piece, like a kilim that you wouldn't dream of laying on the floor, or Great Aunt Myrtle's antique quilt. However all wall-hung objects should be at least 3ft (93cm) above the stairs so that no one can get caught on them while going downstairs.

LIGHTING There needs to be enough lighting on the stairs to allow for safe ascent and descent. A linked switch at the top and bottom of the stairs is helpful to ensure that no one

This landing was an empty space with large windows just waiting for plants, there was no obvious space for the piano elsewhere and the angel was just passing, liked the music and decided to stay. Together, dramatically lit on dimmer switches, they bring a dead space to life. The stairs on the left benefit from the light but they have their own independent source as well.

uses them unlit. Dimmer switches for lights outside the bedrooms allow both you and your children to get up in the night without waking the rest of the family and it is not such a shock to your eyes.

Low-level light switches are a good idea if your children are very young. It means they can turn on the light to go upstairs without your help, with less likelihood of them being intimidated by imagined werewolves loitering in the darkness of their bedroom. Adults can use these low switches just as easily.

FLOOR TREATMENTS AND COVERINGS   Whatever you choose for the flooring of your hall, stairs and landings, it needs to be hard wearing and hide the inevitable heavy traffic to which it is subjected. The most important item on the floor in a family home is an enormous door mat, or even two, one inside and one on the door step. Ideally, the mat inside the main door should be wide enough to take at least two paces in from the door, and should be flush with the carpet or other flooring, so that no one can trip over it. If it is left loose laid it can be lifted and shaken from time to time to dislodge the build-up of dust and dirt and small, precious items caught in and under the matting.

If you choose carpet for your hallway it needs to be specifically designed for hard-wearing areas and to be a neutral colour, not too dark and not too light. Although cheap, sisal is not a good alternative because it is too rough; small children spend a lot of time either on their knees or running about in bare feet, and falling over on sisal can do more than just damage your dignity.

Wooden stair treads in a house may look beautiful but if there are to be children running up and down them consider covering them with carpet. If left painted or varnished, the

noise level will be deafening. Uncarpeted stairs are also very slippery for anyone not wearing rubber soles, and if someone falls down them it could be dangerous. Carpet, when laid, should be fully fitted if possible to avoid the danger of edges to trip up on.

Floor tiles in ceramic, cork or even vinyl all make a good, easy-to-clean surface for an entrance hall. Make sure that whatever you choose it is not too light in colour and does not show the dirt. When stripped, sealed and painted or varnished, wood makes a good floor for a hall as it is warm and easy to clean. However, try to resist the temptation to put down a rug or runner because children tend to dash about in a hall, and it is just too easy to trip and slide. If you have a new wooden floor laid it is worth ensuring that the type of wood you choose will not be dented by stiletto heels.

THE ENTRANCE HALL

This is usually the first place a visitor sees, so it needs to be welcoming and kept as free as possible from family clutter, and anything stored in the hall should not block the flow of traffic. Fitting a smoke alarm to the ceiling is a worthwhile precaution (see Fire Safety p.15).

THE FRONT DOOR When your children are too young to open the door make sure that you always put the door on the latch or take a key with you if you need to go outside to put out the rubbish or whatever. It is very traumatic for everyone if you are suddenly locked out and your small child is inside.

Children love to open the front door to see who is there so it is safer to fit a spy glass low enough in the front door for a child of about six years old to look through before opening the door. Teach them never to open the door to anyone they don't know. For security, have a light fitted outside your porch which you can turn on inside, so that you can see clearly who is at the door after dark.

If you have an entryphone or intercom, it should be out of small children's reach. As they love to play with telephones you may find them letting in complete strangers before you have a chance to get to answer the door yourself.

STORAGE If there is going to be a new baby in the house, it will probably mean a pram or baby carriage as well, and unfortunately the hall is often the only place to keep it. The advent of buggies and strollers which are so much easier to store does mean that the traditional pram is only used for about six months, by which time it should be stored elsewhere or passed on to someone else as quickly as possible.

If you are going to buy a buggy, it is a good idea to think about how and where it is going to be kept before you choose a particular model, because some collapse down more compactly than others. It is best to keep it in a cupboard in the hall or somewhere with easy access to it, so that you resist the

You could adapt the storage ideas, left, for almost any shape or size of hall, so long as the closet is only 18in (46cm) deep. With careful thought about what needs to be accommodated, it will keep any hall tidy. Coat hangers can be used for the adult coats but most children's coats don't need them and if you want to encourage your children to hang up their own coats it has to be as simple an operation as possible or they will end up on the newel post any way. Wellington boots will probably need to be kept somewhere else in case they are put away with wet mud on them. Accessories and sports equipment are hung on the door so that they are easy to put away.

temptation just to leave it lying around. Perhaps there is room to build a tall, shallow cupboard or a long low one, to accommodate this indispensable piece of equipment. A long narrow bench with storage under the seat (see below) could also accommodate a buggy. If there simply isn't anywhere else, a bicycle or hat hook on the wall is better than leaving the buggy on the floor to be kicked or tripped over.

Coats and hats are often kept in an entrance hall; this is a particularly good idea when living with children as most have a habit of dropping everything the moment they walk through the door, especially after a hard day at school, leaving a trail of coats, school bags and shoes as they shuffle through to see what's in the fridge. This often makes it hard for the next person even to open the front door, let alone drop his or her own coat, school bag and cello in the middle of the hall, and tread unperturbed on the first set of abandoned gear en route to see what's on television.

To avoid this scenario you will need lots of hanging space, lots of hooks, and lots of patience to begin with. A family of four people may have as many as twelve coats or jackets hanging up at any one time, not to mention the many small friends who turn up with a coat and leave without it, so ideally a family of four needs a minimum of a dozen hooks. They don't all have to be in the same place as long as the most frequently used coats are in the most convenient position.

For the children's use, put double coat hooks at child height, not less than 4in (10cm) apart, varying the height so that some can be used for long coats and some for jackets and smaller children's coats. Make sure the children can reach them but that they have to stretch up to do so; that way you won't need to move the hooks up so often as they grow. Leave space, too, for young visitors' coats.

Scarves, hats and gloves can all be thrown in a low basket which is kept in the hall for the winter. Then, when they are no longer needed, they can be stored elsewhere.

Frequently there is a space under the stairs which can be put to more profitable use.

If there is only enough space for storage, use it to its

ABOVE Simple wooden strips with turned wooden knobs for hooks provide space for hanging all sorts of things, apart from coats that are stored in a cupboard elsewhere in the hall.

RIGHT The space under these stairs is given over completely to the children's paraphernalia. There isn't enough room for the whole family's coats in the entrance hall, and it is difficult for adults to reach into this low sloping cupboard. There are bright red baskets for hats and gloves, and hooks for coats on both sides of the cupboard so there is room for everyone and a few extra as well. The cupboard is well-lit to find that stray shoe that is hiding at the back. The floor is kept clear in the middle and shoes are only stored around the edges.

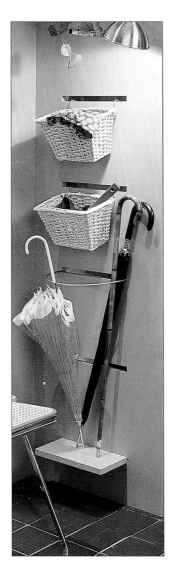

ABOVE Painted bicycle baskets hanging from slats cut out of the end of a coat closet on hooks, provide extra storage and look attractive.

RIGHT This entrance hall incorporates many features designed with children in mind which are unobtrusive but successful. The coconut matting is large enough to turn a buggy on so that muddy wheels can be cleaned, and there is space for visitors to leave their buggies on the mat. Letters are collected in a box on the back of the front door that is hard for a small child to open. School bags and shoes are kept under the blue iron bench which can be covered with a colourful durry to hide the clutter. There are coat hooks at child height on the right hand side and more at the back of the hall.

best advantage by making sure you can reach all the space. This may mean cutting a door at the side of the angled space.

A small cupboard with drawers is more use than a table in a hallway because of the storage space it offers. Don't let it protrude too far, as there must be enough space for the family to move past it easily.

A long narrow bench with storage in or under the seat is ideal for storing shoes and boots. If you get your children into the habit of taking their shoes off as they walk into the house and putting them in a specific place, you will not be faced with the chore of looking for a stray shoe that is found 45 minutes later in the second drawer of the desk, and your floors will stay a lot cleaner. The lid of the bench should be fitted with rubber stops to make sure that fingers don't get pinched when the lid is lowered. Only keep shoes that are used daily in it because it will soon fill up and make everything harder to find. If you tend to have a lot of shoes and boots in the hall, another idea for storing them is in a wicker laundry basket. This is particularly useful when the shoes are damp and muddy as the mud can drop through onto sheets of newspaper when it dries out. If you have space, put it in front of a radiator.

Keep a letter rack on a high shelf in the hall, too high for very young children to reach in case they decide that hiding big sister's exam results behind the sofa would be fun. When your children are older make sure they can reach the letter rack, and use it, so that mail doesn't go astray.

LEFT Although there is little natural daylight in this hall, the combination of light colours throughout and the large, framed mirror create a feeling of airy space, that isn't diminished even when the folding pool table is set up for a game. The problem of dirty finger marks on light paintwork is simply solved by painting the area below the dado rail in a marble effect, echoed on the mirror frame, which is not difficult to produce and hides marks very successfully, it has also been glazed to make it easy to clean. Although light-coloured flooring in an entrance hall is not always practical, these vinyl tiles are very easy to clean, and anyway most of the mud will be wiped off on the coconut matting that spans the area of the entrance hall that you can see reflected in the mirror.

BELOW This large central hallway has been sensibly organised to provide lots of extra playing and storage space and is a good place for a piano which might otherwise dominate a family or living room. The parquet floor has proved irresistible for bikes, roller skates and skateboards – these and other large toys are kept under the stairs that lead down into the hall and there is plenty of room in the closets for all the family's coats and sports equipment, so that the space can be completely emptied except for the piano. As this is on an inside wall the music doesn't penetrate outside to cramp the shy pianist's style, and at least the neighbours don't have to listen to Für Elise twenty times a night.

Large hats can be very bulky to store but they can look decorative hanging on hooks in a cluster on the wall. A mirror is useful and helps to enlarge and lighten a narrow hallway. It could either be a full length one hung 1ft (30cm) above the floor so that bikes don't run into it, or a smaller one hung low enough for children as well as adults to look into. It needs to be firmly attached to the wall and given enough light to reflect properly.

STAIRCASES

The staircase is a potentially hazardous place for the whole family; children rarely manage to reach the age of five without having fallen down some stairs, so they need to be treated with caution. Stair gates at the top and bottom are essential when your children are very small – babies can climb stairs long before they can walk, but they take a lot longer to learn how to come down safely.

There should be hand rails on one or both sides of the stairs. If you have a sheer drop on one side it is important to add the upright posts of a balustrade, or bannister as it's usually known. Although your own children will get used to holding onto the wall at the side of the stairs other children coming to play may well trip and fall off the edge.

Some wooden stair treads are designed to be left uncovered, but they can be rather slippery for children who run around in socks (see above).

SPIRAL STAIRCASES Though very attractive and space-saving, a spiral staircase is a problem with young children because it is difficult to use a stair gate with it, and the rails are often wide enough apart for a child to slip through. Older children tend to treat them as indoor climbing frames, while younger ones find the steps difficult to negotiate, especially coming down. However, if you have got one the only answer is to escort children up and down it until such time as you feel that they can go by themselves, aware of the dangers.

LANDINGS

If your landings are quite large but generally just wasted space, they can be put to good use for extra storage, another bathroom or even an office, as long as the person using it doesn't mind children thundering past up and down while he or she is working. Make sure that the landing isn't draughty before you set up your work station, and that you really have enough space to work in; if your work spills over onto the stairs themselves it may become a potential hazard.

Shelves for paperback books don't take up much space and can take up any overflow. If the shelves are built in and arranged around a window it will make the space more interesting to look at but be sure the window is childproofed if your children are young, as the shelves may act as a ladder.

Cupboards with 5in (12cm) deep adjustable shelves (see p.31) can hold lots of things that are difficult to store, without their being any visible difference to the size of a small landing. Rackets, balls and other sports equipment, wrapping paper, ribbon and sticky tape, shoe polish and brushes – in fact all sorts of small or flat items could find a permanent home at last.

The rooms in this house were small enough to warrant opening up the whole floor to make the hall, kitchen, dining room and living room into one big area. This allows the graceful curve of the stairs to be a feature in its own right, and the clever storage of the bicycles becomes a work of art. Carefully chosen objects are displayed on the stairs, with unbreakable items on the lower shelves.

LEFT *A kitchen which leads out into the garden is ideal for a family with young children. The paved area just outside is perfect for meals in fine weather as the food does not have to be transported far; the all-weather garden furniture has a matching table at the far end of the garden that can be brought onto the terrace to provide extra space for summer parties.*

The sink overlooks the garden which means an adult can supervise small children playing outside while cooking or washing up, and there's a pretty view as well.

The garden end of this kitchen/ dining room has been given a glass roof to provide extra light for the whole room.

The kitchen, with all its warmth and bustle, is the heart of the home, and the whole family is drawn to it. A family kitchen should be large enough to accommodate everybody's needs safely and comfortably, as well as being designed to look attractive, so that the primary functions of preparing and cooking food can continue alongside, but unimpeded by, the activities of other members of the family.

Although the kitchen is the hub of the household, it is also the most dangerous room in any home, and although most people are aware of this, there are still thousands of horrific but avoidable accidents every year, especially involving children under five. Sensible forethought will help you protect your children from themselves . . . and your belongings from your children.

Remember that while 'childproof' aids are very helpful, you cannot sit back and rely on them entirely. Some children will work out how to open a fridge lock long before they are supposed to be able to. Some children are far more inquisitive than others, but even the most apparently incurious child may suddenly decide one day to see what the floor polish tastes like. Follow your instincts and be aware of the particular problems that you have in your kitchen, then deal with them in the appropriate way, sooner rather than later. The different safety aids are discussed where relevant below.

This cleverly designed counter top has a raised rim so that spilt liquids cannot run over the edge, but simply pool on the top, making it much easier to clean. The counter top itself has been made up from hundreds of individual off-cuts of wood that have been evenly planed so that the edge of the grain shows and covered with a polyester resin that makes a perfectly flat and hard-wearing surface.

ABOVE AND BELOW Two chair designs which are very difficult to tip back on because they do not have conventional chair legs. The chair below is based on a classic 1920s Bauhaus design.

When your children are very young it is natural for them to be with you most of the time when awake, so the kitchen often gets taken over as a part-time playroom. Older children tend to do their project work at the kitchen table so they can bombard you with different questions about the Himalayas, and teenagers see it as a golden opportunity to air their problems to a captive audience. To avoid allowing young children near the cooking area it is essential that the design incorporates some kind of natural barrier, for example, a peninsular or island unit behind which they are safe when cooking is in progress.

A small kitchen need not necessarily be a problem for a family if it is well-designed, so that two people are able to prepare, cook or clear up at the same time. If your family is young and your kitchen is too small to allow everyone to congregate there while meals are being prepared, it needs to have an adjoining space for the children so that they can be easily supervised but safe from the hazards of cooking.

One solution is to knock an open viewing hatch or window through to the adjoining room, like a large dining room serving hatch. (If the play area doubles as a dining room the hatch can actually be used for serving – see p.52.) Folding shutters or sliding doors close off the room when supervision isn't required. Having an adjoining room also helps to stop the person preparing meals or cleaning up after them from feeling isolated and resentful – this is particularly important when older children are required to start pulling their weight in the kitchen. It also means that toys needn't come into the kitchen at all – although they inevitably will.

DESIGNING YOUR KITCHEN

The science of ergonomics studies the relationship between people and machines, and the environments that are adapted or chosen for them. The importance of ergonomics to kitchens has been recognized by architects and designers for many years; it is applied to things as the height of the counters and the wall cupboards. If you and your partner are very different in height then some counters should be higher than others as it is very uncomfortable working on a surface that is not the right height for you and is bad for your back. Adult height worktops are of course going to be much too high for your children for many years so it is important to have a sturdy plastic step stool kept in the kitchen just for your children's use. It needs its own accessible storage space in the bottom of a cupboard as nothing should be left on the kitchen floor to be tripped over, and your children can be trained to get it out and put it away themselves.

If they are going to help with cooking, most children find a kitchen table more comfortable to work on as it is lower. If you are planning a peninsula unit which will also be used as a breakfast bar with stools, a good idea is to have a lower shelf built out from one side of the unit. Children can then use it for cooking or to sit at on low stools which are safer than the usual high bar stools. This is particularly useful for a small kitchen which does not have room for a table.

The layout of your kitchen is very important with children. Make sure that there is an unbroken cooking line between the stove and the sink, with the fridge very close by. You must be especially careful if there is a through route to another part of

RIGHT As much width as possible has been given to this long narrow kitchen/dining room by building in cupboards with shelving only 6in (30cm) deep the whole length of the right hand wall. An insignificant amount of space is lost in the room and the floor to ceiling cupboards provide ample space for most items. Almost everything in a kitchen store cupboard is less than 6in deep so this sort of storage is ideal, because items are only stored one deep making things easy to find. With adjustable shelving wasted space is kept to a minimum.

The kitchen area is divided from the eating area by the peninsular unit in the foreground which provides deeper cupboards for crockery, saucepans and other large items. The cupboard at the dining end is also deeper to accommodate a television which can be seen from anywhere in the kitchen, but which can also be locked away behind doors along with the alcohol.

In order to avoid the piles of important information that accumulate in a kitchen, one of the closed cupboards at the end has eight magazine files, two for each member of the family, so that their belongings can be scooped up and kept for them to be sorted out when the box is full. Important reminders are kept in these boxes too.

RIGHT Having children doesn't mean that you can't have anything that is fragile or beautiful in your kitchen, it just means that you need to keep them out of reach until your children are old enough to treat them with respect, at about 20 years!

FAR RIGHT The warm, fresh colours combined with the hanging baskets, dried flowers and the stencilling on the walls create a summery atmosphere in this kitchen all year round. The pink and white theme is a wonderful background for the cottage china, shown in detail, left, and the green chairs. The baskets above the table are hanging from butchers hooks that have had their sharp ends knocked off for safety. The table is an ideal height for children to cook on, with the pastry cutters hanging ingeniously close at hand.

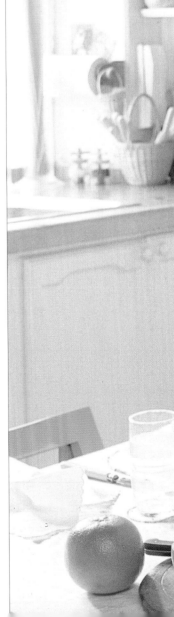

the house, perhaps from the garden or a play area, to avoid being crashed into by a zooming two-year-old while you are holding a pan of boiling water. It helps if the stove top, microwave and oven are accessible for an older child to use, under supervision, while standing on a step stool (see above). This may need some advance planning if you are designing your kitchen while your child is still an infant.

FIRE PREVENTION Cooking accidents are the most common cause of fires in the home, so you should always have a fire blanket and a fire extinguisher in the kitchen. The fire blanket should be used for pan fires and kept near the door, rather than by the stove top, as you might think. This is to make sure you can reach it safely if something does catch fire on the stove. The fire extinguisher should also be kept near the door, so that you don't find yourself trapped.

DECORATION

A priority in any kitchen is that it is easy to clean. This is obvious in a family kitchen that is bound to be used a lot, often by fast-moving, sandwich-holding streaks of lightning. If you are going to hang wallpaper, make sure it is washable, as regular wallpaper is too hard to keep clean. On the whole paint finishes are more practical in a kitchen. Vinyl silk emulsion paint (latex semigloss) washes easily so is particularly good for a kitchen. The choice of colour is yours; unfortunately, there is no perfect colour that hides all the

finger prints, felt tip pen marks and food stains. However, paint finishes such as rag rolling, sponging and stencilling make the finger prints harder to see and can look wonderful.

One way to decide on a colour is to choose one that is warm or fresh but not too dominant, and let the walls be a simple backdrop for the collection of objects that are kept and used in the kitchen, allowing them to provide colour and texture. Another route is to be definite about the colour of the walls and collect everything else to suit it. This system is fine if you are starting from scratch but isn't practical if you already have lots of equipment which doesn't match your chosen colour scheme.

The kitchen is a good place for displaying your children's precious works of art. Rather than taping up paintings which soon begin to curl at the edges or putting up pasta collages from which bits descend onto the floor, you could mount them in a few simple clip-frames of various sizes and hang them on the wall. It makes them look much more important, preserves them well, and the children won't mind so much if you decide to ring the changes from time to time. If it is difficult to hang them in your kitchen, this method could equally well be used in a downstairs bathroom or passageway, or in the playroom.

THE KITCHEN CLOCK A clock is important in a kitchen, which is a good place to practise telling the time. A wall-mounted clock in a prominent position is best. For this reason a clock with an analogue rather than a digital system is best, as it takes a while for children to realize that 3:35 is the same as twenty-five to four. The numbers should be clear – Roman numerals are not a good idea unless your children can already tell the time.

BULLETIN BOARDS Many people keep a bulletin board in the kitchen, along with a week- or month-to-view calendar, for shopping lists, invitations, dental appointments, postcards from Grandma and messages that the family needs to leave for each other. These boards can be bought commercially, or can be made from thick cork tiles either mounted in a frame or glued onto the wall. A piece of soft board covered in coloured felt, with ¾in (9mm) wide elastic criss-crossed over it looks very good and reduces the need for drawing pins. It is true that bulletin boards can become rather cluttered and untidy; if this worries you, position it on the inside of a cupboard door.

SOUND PROOFING Because all the surfaces are very hard in a kitchen there is nothing to absorb the noise, which can be considerable. You will notice the difference if you add curtains or blinds to the windows and perhaps a cushion or two to chairs or stools. If this is inappropriate just find something soft, flame-retardant, washable or disposable, to put up as a wall hanging.

LIGHTING

If you eat as well as cook in the kitchen you can make a visual division between the cooking and eating areas by having separate lighting systems with dimmer switches in each area. This means you can shade off the working area when you are eating by switching off or dimming the lights there.

The clean lines of these rooms give them a feeling of spacious stylishness, with the areas open enough to give the advantages of a combined kitchen/dining room, yet far enough apart to separate the two functions totally. The cooking debris can be hidden away during dinner parties, but equally the children can be stopped if they throw their food at each other while an adult is in the kitchen. The cupboards are rag rolled in a fingermark-proof grey and the view to the garden ensures that any argument on the climbing frame can be nipped in the bud before it goes too far.

The table needs to have a good light source over it so that you can see clearly what you are eating. The best and most attractive system is two low voltage recessed fittings in the ceiling about a foot apart over the centre of the table. These are quite expensive to buy and instal but cheap to maintain and run.

If your children habitually play or work in the kitchen they need good lighting over the whole area from different sources, otherwise they will be playing in their own shadows, especially when they are young and spend a lot of time on the floor. Track lighting with adjustable spots gives great flexibility, but if you have a low ceiling, adjustable recessed fittings at regular intervals look better and keep clean longer. The number of fittings depends on the size and shape of the kitchen, so take the advice of a good retailer for this. Fluorescent lighting is just too cold for a kitchen.

Task lights on the counters can either be under-cabinet lighting in strips or small spots, or lights from the ceiling. The important thing is for the whole area to be lit and that you are not working in your own shadow.

HEATING

The kitchen should be a warm place. Because the stove and in some places the central heating boiler are situated there, it usually is, and indeed can become too hot sometimes in summer. However, it is still very important that there are enough radiators or other sources of heating to avoid being greeted by a cold kitchen first thing in the morning – or in the small hours when you have to go and warm up the baby's bottle.

Underfloor heating is no longer as expensive to instal as it was and if you are putting in a new floor it is worth looking into (see below). Young children spend a lot of time on the kitchen floor, so make sure that there are no draughts coming in where you want them to play. If they get cold, they will be uncomfortable and will gravitate towards the warmer area, probably too near the stove.

Low level electric heaters fixed to the base boards provide useful booster heating for chilly moments, especially when other sources of heating are turned off.

FLOORING

There are relatively few practical floorings for the kitchen because it gets an enormous amount of traffic, especially if it leads to the garden. As well as being subject to spills and soakings, the floor needs to hide muddy footprints and the mixture of biscuit and apple juice smeared into it at regular intervals, so that you don't have to wash it more often than you need.

You can insist that your children wipe their feet when they come into the house, and put a large mat there for the purpose. This may even sink in eventually, but explaining it to the dog or the kitten is a thankless task, not to mention Fred from up the road who seems to spend an enormous amount of time in your house leaving a trail of mud from his crepe-soled shoes. So the answer is first to get the children to take their shoes off as a matter of course, and then when they forget for the *nth* time to make sure it doesn't show too much.

This convenient work tray kept in the kitchen means that the homework or drawing can be easily moved when lunch is ready.

VINYL SHEETING AND TILES These are probably the most popular floor coverings for kitchens. They are easy to keep clean – no waxing is needed – they are very hard wearing as a rule and there are lots of different patterns to choose from. Sheet vinyl has the advantage of being less vulnerable to water damage than tiles. Make sure that the design you choose is non-slip and doesn't show the dirt too easily.

WOODEN FLOORS These are very good in kitchens. They can be sanded, stained, stencilled or painted. They are smooth and warm and as long as they are well sealed they are very easy to keep clean. From time to time you will need to reseal them, especially in heavily-used areas. Some people use maritime varnish, the sort used on yachts, because if it can withstand being pounded by the sea in a Force 10 gale it ought to be able to withstand your children. If you are installing a new wooden floor, a hard wood is most durable.

CORK TILES Cork tiles are easy to lay and are ideal for small children to play on. Once sealed, they are very easy to keep clean, (the dirt doesn't show anyway), they are warm to the touch and comfortable underfoot. You can get ready-sealed tiles, but for a family kitchen it is wise to seal them with a further two coats of polyurethane varnish for extra hard wear.

This cosy, garden level kitchen is always warm because of the stove and the low ceiling, while the way it is decorated gives it a comfortable farmhouse feel. The two sinks allow washing up to be separated from cooking and preparation which makes it easier for two people to cook and clear up at the same time. A walk-in larder to the left, out of shot, contains a large fridge and freezer, and adjustable narrow shelves for jars and bottles, above wider shelves and bottle racks. Behind the camera a family room leads to the garden (see p.74) so that all the children's daytime needs are centralized in the one area. The adjustable lights over the counter mean that no-one need ever work in his or her own shadow.

When the children are older cork tiles could be replaced perhaps with ceramic tiles with underfloor heating.

The only drawback with pure cork is that because they are tiles any large amount of water that seeps in between them may get under the seal and turn the tiles white at the edges or even lift them from the floor. This is not a problem with ordinary cleaning, only if the dishwasher leaks while you are away for the weekend. However, a new type of cork tile backed with vinyl combines the advantages of both flooring materials and is less vulnerable to water damage.

CERAMIC OR QUARRY TILES These look wonderful, are very durable and usually very easy to keep clean. But they are hard and cold, so may not be the solution in a kitchen. They increase fatigue to the back and feet because there is no 'give', they are unsuitable for small children playing on the floor, and a plate will break on them even if it is dropped from a height of six inches – not to mention a child's head.

Many people are prepared to put up with the problems of breakages and coldness underfoot because they like ceramic tiles so much to look at. If you feel this way too then think of having another flooring such as cork tiles (above) whilst the children are young, then save up for a ceramic floor with underfloor heating later.

EQUIPMENT

Positioning and choice of kitchen equipment is very important with growing children around. Most children love to cook and if you encourage them from an early age then they will benefit and so will you. This does need your time and patience; supervision is vital to the safety of your children while they are using the equipment and vital to your sanity when the flour is being 'mixed' haphazardly with the egg.

HOBS OR STOVE TOPS Any controls should be on the top not in front, to lessen the chance of inquisitive fingers turning on the rings unnoticed. Small children should be taught from as early as possible that the stove top is hot and dangerous. A ceramic hob can be a hazard with children in the home. Children don't always notice the warning light, so they may burn themselves on residual heat and the hob can be difficult to clean if the food gets burnt on after over-enthusiastic stirring, especially of sugary ingredients.

When you are cooking, always turn the handles of saucepans inwards. You can fit a guard that helps prevent children pulling pans down onto themselves, but it could be more of a hindrance than a help as you may catch the bottom of a full, hot pan on the edge of it while lifting it off the stove and thereby spill the contents, possibly causing burns to yourself or your child if she's nearby. In any case you should never leave a small child alone in a kitchen when you have something on the stove. If someone comes to the door or the phone rings, take your small child with you to answer it. Never store foods above or near the hob that children are particularly interested in, like snacks or cookies.

OVENS A glass-fronted oven with an internal light makes cooking much more fun for a child as you can see if the cake is rising (or not). Some oven doors can get extremely hot and

The window seat in this kitchen is a lovely place to eat breakfast in the sun, and also provides a comfortable seat for a visitor to chat to the cook. The windows were kept shut and locked when the children were very small but now they are older they are sometimes used for a quick exit into the garden (which is on the same level) when searching questions are asked about the completion of homework. The vinyl floor hides any biscuit dropped on the floor and missed by the dog. Behind the camera there is a hatch leading through from the kitchen into the dining room, so that meals are just as convenient there.

This is one example of the different types of childproof cupboard latch which are available. Make sure that you get the right ones to suit your cupboards, and that you replace them promptly if they become ineffective. It is usually safe to remove them when a child is about five years old.

small children need to be warned and kept away from them. An eye level oven is good from this point of view but if it is combined with a grill it makes it hard for them to use until they are almost as tall as you. However, the lower oven/grill of a wall-mounted double oven is usually just the right height for a child.

MICROWAVE OVENS These can be very useful for a busy family that may want to eat at different times and eat different things. The main drawback as far as children are concerned is that both the bowl or plate the food is being cooked in, and the food itself, get very hot so fingers and mouths are often burnt as a result. Make sure there's a pair of really efficient oven gloves kept handy solely for use with the microwave and make sure everyone uses them as a matter of course. Family members get used to this very quickly but young visitors need to be alerted. If you feel your children are old enough to cope easily without burning themselves, a microwave could be installed within their reach, free-standing at the back of the counter so plates or cups can be removed easily onto the counter in front of it.

DISHWASHERS There is no excuse for a teenager or even a younger child to leave the kitchen in a mess with dirty plates piled in the sink if you have a dishwasher, although emptying it has taken over from doing the washing-up as a source of family conflict in many households. A 12-place capacity machine is ideal for a family of four to six people. Find one that makes the least noise, so that when it's on you aren't all shouting above it. Consumer publications are a good source of research for this. One alternative is use the timer switch (or buy a socket-mounted one if your machine doesn't have an integral timer) and do your dishes in the middle of the night, taking advantage of cheaper electricity rates.

Ask your children to time you and see if it takes you more than five minutes to empty the dishwasher. If it does you need to rethink your storage of everyday equipment and use the time you have saved on something you enjoy – or something else you should be doing.

Dishwashing powder, salt and rinse aid need to be kept out of reach of small children. Don't let small children near the door of the dishwasher when the powder is in the dispenser as they may put it in their mouths and it is highly abrasive. Try to prevent your children walking on the door when it is open; it's a great game but it doesn't do the machine any good.

WASHING MACHINES AND TUMBLE DRIERS In many countries it is illegal to keep these appliances in the kitchen for reasons of hygiene. It certainly is a good idea to position them elsewhere if you possibly can, as much for the noise as anything: if you have the space, the ideal place is a separate utility room (see p.50).

REFRIGERATORS AND FREEZERS The bigger the better is definitely true for both these appliances if you have a growing family. If you only have space for a refrigerator under the worktop, get the largest capacity that you can fit in. You may find that the fridge you have in your kitchen can be supplemented by another one in a utility room or elsewhere that can be used mainly for drinks and bulk cold storage.

As tables and counter tops are the right height for a small child to hit her head on and some of the corners are extremely sharp, fitting these simple plastic covers guards against the worst of these knocks.

If you also keep a freezer in the kitchen, use a larder fridge so that you don't duplicate the ice-making compartment. Some modern fridges have an external dispenser for ice cubes and iced water which are excellent for a large family. There are fridge locks on the market which can deter the inquisitive fingers of the very young who like to turn the fridge down to 2 or sample a little bit of each of its contents. However, these locks do not have a very long life. Some refrigerators have transparent doors – this facility has a lot to be said for it if your children take a long time deciding which flavour of yoghurt they want today.

Chest freezers are a potential hazard because they are a good place to hide, and you may not realize this has happened if the freezer is in a utility room, basement or garage. Keep it out of bounds and explain why. Many freezers are fitted with locks – don't leave the key in the lock and don't let young children know where you keep it. You can buy a freezer alarm that sounds when the freezer has been left open and the temperature is beginning to rise. The device needs to be positioned carefully but it is useful if your freezer is used by the whole family so may be left open, or is not in the kitchen.

ELECTRIC KETTLES AND COFFEE MAKERS When your children are small your kettle should have a coiled wire so that it doesn't dangle over the edge of the counter for a child to pull at. Never leave the electric wire plugged into the socket but not into the appliance – if a child gets hold of it and puts it in her mouth she could be electrocuted. A guard is now available that keeps the kettle at the back of the counter each time after use.

The kettle guard ensures that the kettle is always kept at the back of the work top.

SINKS Even if you have a dishwasher, the kitchen sink seems to be in constant use so it is a good idea to have it positioned by a window if at all possible, overlooking the garden if you have one. Make a feature of it with pretty, washable curtains or a blind, or hang a basket of trailing plants like lemon-scented geraniums, ferns, tradescantia and even annuals like lobelia and nasturtium. If the sink is by the window you can supervise small children while they are playing at the same time as scrubbing the new potatoes, and you also have a view which lessens the feeling that you spend all your waking hours at the cooker or sink.

Two sinks are sensible as they make cooking and clearing up at the same time much easier. It is a good idea to have one sink large enough to be able to wash a grill pan or oven dish easily. One of the sinks could include a waste disposal unit (but see below).

WASTE DISPOSAL Rubbish is both fascinating and potentially dangerous for small children. Keep the kitchen rubbish behind a childproofed door so that your child cannot put her hand into the bin and cut herself on an empty can or deposit the expensive Swiss watch that you just removed while you were washing your hands.

The usual place for a bin to be sited is under the sink. This is normally a good place for it, but when two of you are cooking or clearing away you may clash at sink and bin, so if you have space it is helpful to have another bin in a different part of the kitchen. If it is impossible to have this bin behind a door then train the family to put any sharp things into the bin

Large wicker baskets fitted on to runners make interesting alternatives to drawers. As the area beyond the sink in this unusually shaped unit is a play area, the bottom two baskets are used exclusively for kitchen toys, and the ones above store tea towels, and other light items that are not dangerous or precious. The cupboard in the centre is childproofed.

under the sink. Swing top or pedal bins are the easiest to use as you can do the whole operation with one hand. However, swing tops are also tempting to young children for use as a 'post box' while your back is turned, which is why you should position them in a cupboard.

A waste disposal unit is very useful but dangerous for small children and they must be warned never to use it. It is essential that the switch is out of reach, possibly even in a childproofed cupboard above the counter. If you haven't already got one and your children are small buy a sink with a 3½in (89mm) wide outlet, so that you have the option to fit one later. Bear in mind that a waste disposal unit is not a good idea if your home is not on the main drainage system – in many places you are not allowed to fit one if you have a cesspool or septic tank.

A waste compactor squeezes the rubbish so that you can fit more into your garbage can. It is a useful gadget for a large family, but it is also possible for an under-five to fit inside it, with obviously terrible results. It is better not to use it at all until your children are over that age and, if you have one already, to keep it locked away for that period.

COOKING UTENSILS With children in the house, it pays to double up on some of the common utensils like rolling pins and potato peelers so that two people can roll out or peel vegetables together. You can't have too many wooden spoons: some with short handles are useful as children find long ones unwieldy. Plastic mixing bowls rather than stoneware or glass ones are safer and lighter for the children's use.

Portable weighing scales are easier for a child to use than those that are attached to the wall, as you can bring them down to the child's eye level for accurate measuring. A jug container reduces the likelihood of spillage between weighing and mixing. Cup measurements avoid this problem altogether, of course. A clear plastic cookery book holder helps keep their cookery books cleaner – and yours.

THE TELEVISION It is a personal choice whether you have a television in your kitchen, there are both good and bad sides to it. On one hand, you can control the spread of food around the house because there is no reason to take it anywhere else. On the other hand, mealtimes might be the only time of day that the family is all in the same place at the same time, so many people feel that the television should give way in favour of conversation. If you do have a television in the kitchen, make sure it can be watched from the cooking area as well as the eating area. It could be wall-mounted on an extending arm so that it can be viewed from different angles.

Once children are over five, keep the television, the video and the remote control within reach. Although it may mean more arguments about what and when to watch, it does mean less scraping of chairs across the floor to turn it on or change the channels. Before that age, keep them out of reach. It is embarrassing to discover that your video repairer has found half a peanut butter sandwich jamming up the works.

THE TELEPHONE A telephone extension in the kitchen is invaluable. A wall-mounted telephone out of reach of a small child but within reach of the cooking area means that you can keep stirring the scrambled eggs while you're arranging for the babysitter to turn up half an hour earlier, enabling you to have a peaceful bath before taking a client out to the opera.

THE ENTRYPHONE OR INTERCOM As you spend a lot of time in the kitchen it is a good place to have the receiver for your front door intercom. If your home is on more than one floor, you could have another receiver upstairs which could serve a dual purpose as an internal intercom. Make sure you instal one with a separate internal intercom control otherwise the whole street will know it's supper time.

FURNITURE

TABLES If you have enough space to have a table in your kitchen, whether you like it or not it will have many other uses, quite apart from meals. It needs to be very stable: this is an instance where getting a new one may be the only alternative if it isn't. Of course, if it is your floor which is uneven then wedges under the table legs are the only alternative to having your whole floor levelled. Either way, if the table rocks it will drive you mad every time a drink spills.

The table top should wipe clean easily with a damp cloth or be covered with a thick plastic or PVC cloth that is hard for a cross or mischievous toddler to pull off. Keep the cloth in place with several double-sided sticky pads. If your table is square or rectangular, you may like to fit rounded plastic edging to the corners.

If the table is in the centre of the kitchen you need at least 2ft 6in (85cm) space around it. If space is a problem you may find a table with a removable or extendable central leaf is a good solution, the leaf to be used to extend capacity only when you are entertaining. If space is at a premium in your kitchen or if you have a small child and the kitchen is one of

This large kitchen has a French feeling to it, its spacious style emphasising the central importance of good cooking and civilized meals in family life. It is a kitchen for all seasons – one set of French doors leads into a heated conservatory, the other directly into the garden itself. The stained glass surrounding both doors gives the only strong colours in the room, and the light shining through them casts a sunny yellow glow across the wooden floor whatever the weather.

The main kitchen working area with an Aga to cook on is out of shot in the foreground, as are two comfortable sofas, a chair and a television, so that all the family activities can take place in the one room and no one need feel left out. Two tables mean that while one is being used for food preparation or meals, homework, needlework or other activities can carry on undisturbed on the other. There is a utility room and a wine cellar leading off the kitchen.

These adjustable stools are incredibly useful, as they are light and easy to carry, with a large height range, but because they have three rather than four legs they might tip a small child onto the floor so are best kept for the over fives.

the main play areas, a gate-leg table with two folding leaves which can be tucked away under the counter top when not in use (along with folding chairs), provides the maximum amount of clear floor space.

You will find yourself feeding and looking after other people's children so it is a good idea to have a table that can seat more than just your own family. Your friends may produce children at the same time as you, and even if they don't you are bound to discover at least one like-minded couple on the PTA with children the same age as yours, so that what used to be a simple supper for four is now a lunch for eight or ten. A round table with a central pedestal looks elegant but is also very useful for a family as extra people can be fitted in easily round it and nobody ends up with a table leg. If your kitchen is a large enough space, it is preferable to use it for entertaining other families with children, rather than a separate dining room. As it is easier to clean, it is much more relaxing for everyone: your guests don't have to spend the entire time on their knees under the table apologizing for their messy children and scrubbing helplessly at your carpet.

Birthday parties can pose a real problem when your table seats eight and Elizabeth insists on inviting the whole class. Apart from alternative strategies – like having a picnic in the garden, or clearing a space and sitting them all down on the floor, or having a buffet tea, providing each child with a cake box and letting them help themselves – you could invest in a sheet of chip board, plywood or conti-board that is larger than the table-top but fits the space you have. You can then simply lay it over the existing table, covered with a plastic table cloth. This extra table-top is useful for lots of occasions but you do need to have somewhere handy to stoore it, maybe under a bed if you do not have room in a garage or attic.

BREAKFAST BAR If your table is not near the cooking area you may want to include a breakfast bar in your kitchen, that seats your children and, if you have space, a couple of friends as well. It is not suitable for very small children who can easily topple off high stools (but see p.30 above), but slightly older children love to use one.

CHAIRS Any chairs that children use need to be sturdy and washable. Make sure they are high enough to go with your table, or provide thick washable cushions, with ties to stop them sliding off from underneath wriggling children. The same rule about stability applies to chairs as to tables, but at least with wooden chairs you can even up the legs yourself.

By the time you are a grandparent, you will have lost count of how many times you have said 'Don't tip back on your chair' and explained patiently to your child how it could hurt her and the chair. Yet a moment later, it is being tipped again, without the child even realizing it in many cases. One answer is to find chairs that are designed not to tip back, such as the tubular chrome cantilevered type based on the original Bauhaus designs. These look extremely stylish as well as being practical in this way.

The same problem applies to scraping a chair back from the table, producing that penetrating noise that provokes a groan from the rest of the family and a 'Don't do that, lift it!' from you. You can rectify this problem easily by sticking a coin-sized piece of thick felt to the bottom of the legs of the chairs. It is useful to have at least four folding chairs that you can store nearby for the frequent visitors that children bring home with them. When you choose them try to ensure that they don't collapse too easily and that it is difficult for a child to pinch his or her fingers.

A box bench on castors provides useful toy storage and a lot of seating. The castors make it easier to move out to open the lid. The lid will be quite heavy and needs to have locking hinges at the sides to keep it up when opened, and rubber shock absorbers on the front inside corners to make sure that no one catches their fingers when closing it.

HIGH CHAIRS Like most baby equipment the design of high chairs gets better and better each year. It is best to buy one from a reputable dealer to make sure it's safe, easy to clean, doesn't take up too much space and is preferably portable. There are several Scandinavian designs which are worth searching out as they last a child longer than the average high chair and some convert into normal kitchen chairs.

BOOSTER SEAT When under-fives have reached the stage of resenting the restriction of a high chair, a booster seat allows them to sit at table comfortably and safely. Always strap the seat to the chair, otherwise it might slip.

This converted grain store makes a surprisingly good family kitchen. The stable door out to the courtyard would keep a toddler in, while also letting in a lot of breeze, and everyone in the garden can hear the gong when it's being sounded. The business end of the kitchen is in the old loose box on the other side of the wooden door, which can be shut if necessary, without cutting the cook off from the rest of the family. The gong gets a lot of extra banging just for the fun of it.

Toy cupboards are usually a jumble of which children can only reach the lower half, and what they want to play with is inevitably underneath everything else. Generally speaking parents simply shut the door on the problem until exasperation forces them to do otherwise. Avoid this scenario, and indulge children's natural propensity to climb, by providing an interesting, space-saving platform play store, with puzzles, books and games on the upper deck, and cushions to sit on in the cosy hideaway underneath.

<u>SOFA OR EASY CHAIR</u> Try to find the space for a small sofa or armchair in your kitchen. It is nice to be able to entertain your friends comfortably in a warm family kitchen while you are cooking. Sick children can decamp there too to be close to you, and it's a good place to curl up for a quick story after lunch.

STORAGE

If you use the kitchen for eating as well as cooking, you will all spend a lot of time there, so it is inevitable that some of the children's belongings will start to accumulate. Rather than fighting a losing battle against this, allow for storage when you are planning your kitchen in the first place, or set aside a cupboard just for their use. Storing their things away behind cupboard doors is preferable as they can look untidy, and toys lying about could be dangerous if you trip.

Although the kitchen will probably not be the main playing space, for young children you need quite a large cupboard, as their toys can be very bulky. There will come a time when the cupboard is so full it becomes unusable: this is the time to 'edit' its contents. You will probably find it easier to do this while the children are out. Keep anything that may be precious somewhere else for a while to see if it is missed.

The cupboard under the sink is usually one of the most dangerous places in the kitchen as this is where most people keep household cleaning materials. If you've got young children, try to break this habit. Remove the poisonous cleaning materials and keep them out of reach in a high cupboard closed with a childproof latch.

You need to use childproof latches from the time your child is sitting up, because she will be crawling before long and you need to be ready for her. Find the right sort of latches to fit your kitchen cupboards – there are several different types to suit different designs. Buy a couple of extra sets to replace any that become worn and ineffective.

Children have greatly differing degrees of curiosity – some may be trying to get things out of cupboards from the moment they can wriggle across the floor, others appear to have no interest at all. However it is better to be safe than sorry and keep childproof latches on cupboard doors and drawers until the age of about four – after that age many children can work out how to open them. You may be able to take them off earlier but it is sensible to keep the cupboards containing dangerous or valuable things secure for a lot longer.

Most purpose-built kitchen unit drawers have a catch that stops them from coming out entirely when pulled too vigorously, thereby emptying the contents all over the floor. But if you have something like a beautiful Welsh dresser in your kitchen, or any other item of furniture with drawers, which was not originally designed for kitchen use, it is a good idea to fit drawer stops. Dressers especially tend to have heavy drawers which tip easily and may cause a nasty foot injury if inadvertantly pulled right out.

Store breakable items such as glasses out of reach, but keep the children's plastic or toughened glass tumblers, bowls and plates low down where they can help themselves. Heavy saucepans should be kept as low as possible to ensure that they don't have far to fall if they are dropped. Keep one floor level cupboard available for rummaging by a toddler – fill it with pans, wooden spoons, plastic bowls, jugs and picnic boxes which won't damage or be damaged.

It is worth keeping an atlas and a dictionary in the kitchen on the shelf with the cookery books to resolve escalating arguments about how you spell Euroroa Atol and where it is. A sewing kit kept in the kitchen comes into its own when your oldest should have been at the bus stop two minutes ago, but the button on the waistband of his trousers has just pinged off into the honey.

Try to keep all your potentially dangerous utensils, including sharp knives, out of sight in a drawer with a childproof latch. These would include such things as skewers, scissors, can openers, and, especially, plastic bags. The drawer should have compartments for the different items so that knives can lie flat with the point of the blade facing the back of the drawer. Explain to your child that the items in the drawer are dangerous and might hurt her.

FIRST AID BOX

Keep a first aid box in the kitchen or in the downstairs toilet, if it is somewhere near the kitchen. The box should be childproof and should contain:–

Sharp, round-ended scissors
Various shaped adhesive bandages
Cotton balls
Antiseptic cream/wipes
Tweezers
Insect bite cream
Children's paracetamol (acetominophin) – not aspirin – in liquid form
Thermometer
Sterile, non-stick dressings
Surgical tape

NB Cold water is the best first aid for burns, but an aerosol burn analgesic could also be kept in the first aid box.
Leave space in the box for any other medicines that you regularly use. This means they don't get left around waiting to be put away in the bathroom after you have used them.

If a glass gets broken, carefully sweep up any large pieces and then with a damp wadge or two of kitchen towel wipe all around the area.

UTILITY ROOMS

These wire baskets on wheels are very adaptable in kitchens and utility rooms where maximum storage is essential. You can construct them in different widths so that they fit the space you have, and the baskets themselves come in different depths.

By definition, a utility room is functional rather than decorative, but if you have one, family life runs much more smoothly, and your kitchen will be far less cluttered. It is best if the utility room is as near to the kitchen as possible, preferably adjoining. What you use it for depends very much on its size, but the basic function is usually for laundry.

UTILITY EQUIPMENT

It's obvious that the more children you have the more washing there is, and there may be times when you feel that life is just washing, with some good bits in between. The sorting, washing, drying, ironing and putting away takes large chunks out of people's lives so you need to develop a good system that shortens the process as much as possible.

WASHING MACHINES AND TUMBLE DRIERS   Whatever else you keep in the utility room, these are the essential appliances. It is so much better to keep them out of the kitchen (see p.40), and indeed in some parts of the world it is illegal to have them there.

While a drier cuts down on the ironing, it is as well to remember that many natural fibres shrink even on the low heat setting of the average drier, and need to be air dried instead. This, of course, is the beauty of a utility room – you can fix up a line or better still an old fashioned drying rack on a pulley, and hang the washing inside the house without having to look at it all the time. If the central heating boiler is in the utility room, there will be a constant heat source in winter which will cut down on the use of your drier. If you don't have a utility room, a large airing cupboard built round your hot water tank (see p.121) can double up very well as a drying cupboard, so that you can still hide the washing.

IRONING BOARD AND IRON   With teenage children in the house, it's useful to be able to leave the ironing board up for last minute ironing, but it's depressing – and dangerous – if it dominates your sitting room or kitchen. If it is big enough, a utility room gives you the option to set up a permanent ironing station, but be careful not to let the cable near any water. It is dangerous to leave the iron on the ironing board because it may get pulled off. Instead, fix a wall-holder for the iron in a position handy for the board and the electric socket.

Ironing can be a chore so it's handy to leave space for a portable radio or television in the utility room. A large counter is good for organizing washing and folding clean linen straight from the drier, helping to cut down on the ironing. A counter is also useful for arranging flowers.

THE SINK   A large deep sink with draining facilities around it is important in a utility room. If the sink is low (see p.118), then the children can clean their own paint brushes or fill their own watering cans.

STORAGE   A row of wall cupboards or shelves can help to store all those items, such as shoe-cleaning materials, flower-scissors and household tools, that are dangerous to children so must be kept out of reach, but are also constantly in use. They also provide useful overflow storage for home-made jams and chutneys, and other bulk-bought dry goods. There is no point in under-using these storage facilities – it is the best place to store unsightly but necessary items.

FRIDGES AND FREEZERS This can be a good place to keep an extra fridge and possibly a freezer if you need more space than you have in the kitchen.

DOWNSTAIRS TOILET Some older utility rooms may once have doubled as a downstairs toilet. If you move into a house like this, the toilet should be separated off and an extractor fan installed if the toilet has no direct ventilation. There should always be two doors with a lobby in between separating a toilet from a kitchen.

BABY CHANGING FACILITY The utility room is a good place downstairs to change the baby, so long as it's warm. The counter should be large enough to take the changing mat and also be the right height for you so you don't have to bend too low. There will probably be ample room for storing all the changing equipment. It is a good idea to hang a strategically placed mobile to amuse a young baby; choose one that is pretty in its own right as it can help to make the whole room look more attractive. Ceramic or sea shell wind chimes hung by a window or door provide soothing sounds as well.

THE OUTSIDE DOOR If your utility room has an outside door, it will become the equivalent of a 'mud room' where the family can store their boots and wet weather gear. The dog can also be left to dry off in here, which eliminates muddy paw prints in the house. A boot rack for boots, outdoor shoes and muddy sports equipment helps to keep the mess confined, and if you have room the family bicycles could be stored here on wall hooks.

A flexible storage system like this one can be added to and changed around when your needs change. It is relatively cheap and can be used all over the home.

ABOVE _This room functions_
harmoniously as a playroom
during the day and an elegant
dining room at night. Only
when the children are asleep can
the candles be lit to lend
atmosphere, and the toys that
are still on display add
charmingly to the overall
decoration. Everyday toys are
stored in the cupboards and
drawers, and the large bowls
and candlesticks are put away at
the very top of the dresser except
for dinner parties. With plenty
of space to spare, the table can
be moved about the room
depending on what games are
being played, and can even tip
up on its side and be stored
against the wall if the whole
floor space is needed.

Dining rooms tend to be formal rooms where leisurely meals
can be enjoyed away from the hurly-burly of the kitchen.
With children in the family, many parents relish the chance
to have civilized, adult-orientated meals in a thoughtfully
decorated and furnished dining room, especially when entertaining. However, if your family meals mainly take place in
the kitchen, the dining room may be under-used, especially
during the day. If this is the case, it is worth considering its
potential as a playroom. If it is a necessary combination, in
that you don't have room to eat in the kitchen and also don't
have the space for a separate playroom, it must be designed so
that you don't feel that the children are playing in the dining
room or that you are eating in the playroom.

The room needs to be as close to the kitchen as possible.
An adjoining room is really the best, so that you don't have to
carry heavy trays or push rattling trolleys for miles along
corridors for meals, and your children will be near enough for
you to keep an eye on them when the room is used for play.

In order to make the room work well, there needs to be a
minimum of furniture and a lot of hidden storage space even
for the most bulky toys, such as a doll's cot or toy garage.
Conversely, toys which are attractive in themselves – a classic
doll's house, for instance, or a beautifully crafted wooden
Noah's Ark – can be positioned so that they remain a
decorative featured of the room.

A dining/playroom will mostly be used by small children, as
older children don't need to be near to their parents all the
time, and like the privacy of playing in their bedrooms with
their friends, away from the rest of the family.

RIGHT _This playroom/dining_
room has been transformed for a
children's party by the simple
addition of balloons and
coloured streamers suspended
above the table. As the occasion
is child-centred, there's no need
to put away all the toys, which
add to the jollity of the
decoration.
Since play is the primary
function of this room, the
dresser containing china and
cutlery is fitted conveniently
into an alcove, with fragile items
high out of reach.

FURNITURE

THE TABLE The dining table needs to be easily movable so that it can be pushed against the wall to make more space for play. It could make a good 'house' with the addition of some suitable drapery, so the more adaptable it can be the more it can be enjoyed by your children. If it is a precious table that you really would rather the children didn't go anywhere near, but there's nowhere else to keep it, protect it with an ample PVC cloth, held in place by the clips used by caterers to keep table cloths in place in the open air.

A table with a leaf in the middle is ideal for a family dining room, since it can be extended for meals, but takes up less space during playtime use. A gate-leg table with two large leaves can be pushed right against the wall and takes up very little space. Any kind of extendable table has the added advantage of allowing you at least to seat the five friends your teenage daughter has invited to supper this evening, while you point her in the direction of the kitchen and leave her to work out how to make a pound of minced beef and three tomatoes stretch to eight people.

CHAIRS You need to be able to push the chairs right under the table to leave as much space as possible for play. If any part of the chair is covered in material it needs to be removable and machine washable. It is better, however, if the chairs can simply be wiped clean.

STORAGE

When your children are playing in the dining room they will need to have easy access to their toys and lots of space, and you may want to have somewhere to keep your best cutlery and table linen. Built-in cupboards are the best way of keeping toys out of sight, and if they are carefully designed, they can double as a sideboard. Childproof any drawers or cupboards that contain valuable or dangerous cutlery or china.

If cupboards are not a feasible option a window seat may provide some storage space under it, or you could use an attractive chest or old-fashioned blanket box. Alternatively, keep the toys in easily transportable toyboxes which can be removed to another room for the evening while you are entertaining.

A dining room that has two uses needs to be carefully designed like the ones below. On the left the room is set up to be played in and on the right it is a dining room ready to receive visitors without any evidence of its other use during the day.

There is room for all the toys to be put away, on adjustable shelves to ensure that there is never any wasted space, with one high shelf that is kept for candlesticks etc. This cupboard will need 'editing' sometimes; like any toy cupboard it gets out of hand and a cupboard that is bulging at the seams where the door won't quite close defeats the object. The clock has numbers on it to encourage learning to tell the time.

DECORATION

In this dual purpose room the walls need to be washable so that they don't look shabby too soon. Washable wallpaper is an alternative as long as it is not one that is designed to peel off very easily – it is too tempting for small, investigative fingers. The colour should reflect light so that the room is bright and airy to play in. When it is used as a dining room the atmosphere will mostly be dictated by the lighting you have installed.

WINDOWS If you have tall windows, or glass doors opening on to a garden or balcony, you may want to have full length curtains. But children enjoy long curtains to hide behind, twist themselves up in – and probably pull down on themselves, unless they have been hung with children in mind. Curtains which drape onto the floor are particularly vulnerable as they will inevitably be tripped over, but decorative ties could hold the curtains back in the daytime.

If, however, your windows don't reach the floor it may be better to have window-length curtains, or perhaps Roman blinds. You run less risk of curtains plus rails descending to the floor onto a very confused child who 'hardly touched them, honestly'.

LIGHTING

The lighting needs to accommodate both activities in a dual purpose dining/playroom. There should be plenty of light for playing in and more subtle lighting for eating by. As there would be little space for table lamps and pendant ceiling fittings are not only unatmospheric but mean that a child playing on the floor won't be able to see what he is doing, wall sconces are a good alternative as long as there are enough of them. This depends on the size of the room, but four would probably be the minimum number, and they should be controlled by a dimmer switch.

FLOORS

Some kind of warm, hard flooring is the best for combining play activities and clearing up after meals. The ideal is a wooden floor or some vinyl tiles laid out in an interesting pattern. Carpet is just too difficult to keep clean and toy cars go much further on a smooth surface. Ceramic tiles are too cold and hard and anything accidently dropped from the table stands more chance of breaking.

RIGHT This is the dining room that leads off the kitchen on page 9; it is designed to be a place to entertain in as well as just eat in. The table opens out rather like an envelope to twice its size, easily seating eight people, and the extra chairs are collapsible and kept either side of the fire place.

LIVING ROOMS

LEFT Even though this sumptuous living room is backed up by a playroom upstairs, the children spend a fair amount of time in here and their needs are taken into account. The ottoman in the centre of the room replaces the more conventional coffee table and is lovely to sit on; it has a cover to protect it when all the family is gathered in the living room.

Small but stable occasional tables are carefully positioned by chairs and sofas so drinks are less likely to be spilt, but even so felt-tip pens (and shoes) have been banned from the room and all the furnishings and carpets have been sprayed to protect them against spills.

There are two kinds of living room, ones your children play in and ones they don't. If you are lucky enough to have another room that can be used as a family room, then you can preserve your living room for entertaining or just listening to music or reading, and you can indulge your taste for cream upholstery or misty-grey fitted carpets. Even so, it is wise to spray them with a protective stain-resistant coating, and to ban felt tip pens and food. If you like to keep drinks in the living room, it is safer to keep the bottles and glasses locked away when not in use.

A separate living room really comes into its own when your children are teenagers and you don't want to lurk in the bedroom while they watch *Nightmare on Elm Street* for the fifteenth time. However, while the children are younger you may find the room hardly ever gets used – so be flexible and see if there is another more productive use for the space.

DECORATION AND FURNISHINGS

Whether you use the room for general family use or not, the walls should be washable so that when Great Uncle John comes to tea and your children are showing him how clever they have become at spreadeagling themselves across the sofa with their heads touching the floor and their less than clean feet touching the wall, the smudges can easily be removed after he has gone. For the same reason the floor coverings and the upholstered furniture need to be made stain resistant and, of course, flame retardant. If there are rugs on a hard floor they should be laid over underfelt to stop them slipping (see p.11).

When the curtains are hung in your living room it is worth remembering how children tend to treat them, so rather than constantly haranguing them to leave the curtains alone, it

ABOVE The back half of this through living room is left empty for young children to play in as it leads out into the garden, although few toys are actually kept there as there is a playroom upstairs.

After Sunday lunch with friends all the parents can sit back and safely let their small children play within sight and earshot but not under their feet. For more intimate occasions the double doors can be closed which saves on heating bills.

All the light switches in this house are 2ft 6in (76cm) off the floor so that the children can easily reach the switches.

may be less wearing to reinforce or add more fixings to the curtain rails. Children can't resist pulling or winding themselves up in curtains especially if they are long, and although this should be firmly discouraged, it may happen whether you like it or not, and you may not be in the room to stop it.

FURNITURE

If your living room is close to the kitchen it can be a very good place to nurse children when they are ill, (except when they are vomiting). It enables them to be close to everything that is happening. Most children do not want to stay in bed, in isolation, when they are ill but like to be able to lie stretched out on a sofa where they can sleep comfortably without having their heads at right angles to their bodies. This goes for tired or ailing parents too.

If you have the space, it is better to have two sofas, for comfort and to avoid arguments. A well-designed sofa-bed that is a good-looking piece of furniture in its own right is another obvious alternative, especially if you have limited space and nowhere else for guests to sleep. The television should be comfortably visible from the sofa when you're lying down, and there should be a stable place for a drink near enough for the patient not to be spilled every time she reaches for it. A small, low table is ideal, rather than the floor – a drink on the floor practically guarantees a stained carpet.

Glass coffee tables can be very dangerous; plate glass is not strong enough to hold a child's weight and many bad accidents have occurred after children have been standing or jumping on a glass table. With children around, glass table tops should be made of laminated or toughened glass. If you are thinking of buying one, check with the retailer. But if you have one and are at all uncertain what kind of glass it is, put your glass-topped table away until your children are over the age of five.

Low, occasional tables, with a leg at each corner, placed beside the chairs and sofas are really a better alternative to one central one when there are small children in the home. It leaves more space and means they don't bump into it or hit their heads on the sharp corners so easily. Each chair or sofa needs easy access to a table or cups of coffee end up balanced on the arm of the chair with possibly disastrous consequences.

Architectural glass such as glass doors and shelves should also be made of laminated or toughened glass. If you are not sure what kind of glass is fitted into your door, cover it with safety film. It is inexpensive and quick to apply and keeps shattered glass in place. It is worth the effort for peace of mind, especially if the glass goes near to floor level.

When your children are very young, there are other hidden hazards in living room furniture that you may not have considered. Rocking chairs can pinch small fingers or toes, however careful you are: one child rocking madly on the chair and another one playing on the floor nearby can be a recipe for disaster, especially as rocking chairs have a habit of shifting imperceptibly across the floor. Free-standing book shelves need to be attached to the wall with small L-shaped brackets, so that they can't topple over even if they become a prop in a dare-devil game of climbing Everest on a clear day. Anything precious and breakable, including poisonous plants (see p.162), must be removed or put well out of reach.

Although the children do use this smart town living room for play, clever storage means there is no evidence of the fact, except for the books on the table. The window seat and cupboards on both sides of the fireplace provide ample space for toys used in this room. They are kept in wheeled baskets, so the toys are very easy to pull out and put away again.
The use of the same soft smoky pink on the chair upholstery, wallpaper, curtains and coving bring cohesion to the decoration but the patterns are chosen to show the minimum of dirt.
The rug on top of the carpet is laid over underfelt to stop it from rucking, a problem which is often not appreciated until someone trips over (see p.11).

This enormous living room was part of a warehouse not long ago and the beams provide easily accessible places to hang all sorts of swings and hammocks, even somewhere to keep the odd canoe, out of the way. Although the area is open plan the kitchen is set well back, giving the small children space to roam safely. the sliding doors open directly onto the garden and there is even room for a slide inside for wet days.

The multi-fuel stove, in the centre of the room, heats the whole space efficiently but when lit has a childproof guard around it at all times and of course the fern is removed from the top. Because the space is large it is very flexible; the furniture is on castors and can be moved about to accommodate the needs of the moment. When other children come to play the furniture is moved back out of the way, but for adult visitors, the sofas can be pulled together, around the fire in the winter, at one end of the room.

This New York apartment living room is ideal for a high rise family with surplus energy to burn. Lots of levels, good use of carpet to cushion bumps and deaden noise, and plenty of soft pillows covered in simple white pillow cases which easily wash, provide comfort and excitement in the minimum of space. Wall mirrors reflect light and the world outside while the hammock, which is cleverly suspended from painted builders' ceiling supports, is just sheer fun.

Electrical equipment such as hifis, CD players and video recorders should also be placed well out of reach of small children and all wires should be hidden. If your children are very young, use a video visor so that they can't get their hands stuck in the works.

If you have a piano, keep the lid down so that children's fingers can't get caught trying to close it. If you live close enough to your neighbours for them to be able to hear your family playing, position the piano against an inside wall and place a blanket or acoustic tiles between the wall and the piano; this doesn't make an enormous difference but it helps a bit. The advantage of an electronic keyboard over a conventional piano is that the use of headphones allows for 'silent' practising.

All the furniture in the living room needs to be kept away from the windows, so that your children can't fall against the glass if they slip while climbing on the back of the sofa. If sofas or easy chairs are on castors, place them in non-slip castor cups (available from furniture stores). The furniture will not slide about when pushed and they also protect carpets from heavy pressure marks.

Living room furniture needs to be solid and not easily tipped over; children tend to use it in very imaginative ways but they do not think about the strain they are putting on it – or its adult owners. It needs to be able to withstand a lot, or be strictly out of bounds to that kind of play and provision made for it elsewhere in the home, otherwise it will become a constant battle between you.

STORAGE

When your children are very young, they are always where you are, so the living room is quite likely to be a place where some toys are kept. Toys tend to be spread everywhere while they are being played with, but they should be quite quick to tidy away as long as you limit the number of different items available and that there is somewhere to put them nearby, preferably low to the floor so that there is no excuse for your children not to help.

Remember that as your child grows so do the amount and size of toys, so, unless there is a separate play or family room, be aware that the living room may need to accommodate toys for a good few years. It is unrealistic to think that they will all be taken back to the child's bedroom every night; this sort of rule leads to unnecessary irritation at the time of night when you and the children tend to be most tired. If you don't want to live with a doll's pram, a sit-upon truck and a football as decoration, work out where would be a good place in the room to keep them all, make the storage space as flexible as you can and if at all possible keep it out of sight. Built-in alcove cupboards, window seats, stencilled or stripped pine chests are all ideas which look attractive in themselves when the toys and children have been packed away at bedtime.

HEATING

An open fire or a wood-burning stove is lovely in a living room but it must be surrounded by a guard that entirely encloses the fire-place, and with wall-hooks so that it cannot be pulled over. There should also be enough radiators to warm the room adequately when the fire is not lit.

Mirrors placed over the fireplace are a hazard because people tend to look closely into a mirror which may take them too close to the fire. Instead, hang your favourite painting over the mantelpiece and position the mirror on the opposite wall where it can reflect light from the fire.

LIGHTING

Good lighting can make an enormous difference to the look of a room. A living room is used for lots of different activities so the lighting needs careful thought to allow a well-lit space for whatever your family wants to do, while maintaining the warm, intimate atmosphere that suits the room. One pendant light simply does not provide adequate lighting. Recessed ceiling fittings on a dimmer switch can be attractive; they should be positioned 3ft (93cm) away from the wall and 3ft (93cm) away from each other. Combine them with stable floor-standing lamps which provide a good reading light when positioned behind a sofa or chair. A floor-standing lamp should have a heavy base and no trailing wires to trip over.

Another alternative is to use at least three table lamps lighting different parts of the room. They should have firm bases which are preferably not too heavy. If your children play in the sitting room try to arrange the lighting so that they are not playing in their own shadow. This means having lots of different light sources, at least one in each corner. Wall sconces in alcoves provide useful back-up especially if controlled separately on a dimmer switch.

This childproof fire guard is essential if there are children in the home; it is attached to the wall and has a top so that your paycheck can't be thrown on the fire to see what will happen, and no sparks can fly into the room.

A family room is a room where everyone can congregate comfortably without having to worry too much about shoes on the sofa or having the TV on while doing the mending. A family room enables a separate living room to be kept spruce for entertaining and for quiet pursuits like reading or listening to Bach when no one else wants to. In a family with children, the family room often doubles as the playroom.

The family room should be light with lots of colour in it. Rather than being a poor second decoratively to the living room, it should have a vitality of its own, but it goes without saying that the decoration should be simple and easy to clean, no matter what the age of your children.

The contents of the room need to be flexible enough to develop as your children grow, and nothing in it should be precious, except perhaps the television, video and hifi. A typical item of furniture for the family room is an old sofa that's great to bounce on; perhaps it's a bit ragged at the edges but it doesn't tip over, it makes a wonderful boat, and what's more it's perfect for hiding behind when it's bedtime. It doesn't matter that it's seen better days, that's all to the good.

The walls could be covered with paintings, posters, and interesting things such as a blown-up photograph of dad, taken when he was sitting reading on the beach with his

RIGHT This room is designed not to be a poor second to the living room, but to have a personality of its own. You can really go to town with vibrant colours, and the soft board panels attached to the wall offer endless scope to add to the decorations.
The room is for people to work and play in, with plenty of comfortable seating to watch television for instance. Even so you can't avoid completely the inevitable squabble about who's got the best seat, but some things you just can't win. An exercise bike and a swing seat could provide exercise while watching TV.

This irresistible family room has lots of clever ideas in it which use simple, inexpensive materials in innovative ways. The blackboards and drawing boards fold flat to the wall and the bookshelf is on castors so that it can be wheeled away when swinging and bouncing.

The butcher's hooks in the ceiling have had their sharp points knocked off, but they are strong enough for a child to swing on and there are quite a few for flexibility.

middle-age spread on display. As most of these will be temporary, with lots of changes, they can all be stuck up with blue tac, or there could be a large area of wall covered with cork tiles or soft board panels covered with felt. Any appointments and arrangements can then be pinned on to it the moment they come in through the door, so that there's no excuse for anyone not to remember that Granny is coming to tea today when they'd arranged to go swimming with Kate. If the family room is too far from the outside door then put the board elsewhere or the information will never reach it.

Family rooms can take many forms, from a playroom to a games room, or a place where music is practised and homework done or even a softroom where anyone can go and

few for flexibility.

The bulletin board on the left hand wall is made of carpet tiles and the children's chair is simply made of vegetable racks with a cushion to sit on.

The storage under the window, with a sink for paintbrushes, is designed to accommodate books and different shaped things, with dowels to divide the sections so that everything can be kept upright. Even the weeping fig is in a bin on wheels.

safely fling themselves about to release some energy or get rid of frustration. It should be a room that tries to encompass all of those things, but unless you have unlimited space you will need to decide which one you will get most mileage out of.

THE FAMILY ROOM AS PLAYROOM

A playroom needs to be downstairs if your children are young, near where you are. It can be moved upstairs when they are older. There needs to be ample storage for toys so that everything has its place. Toys need to be easy to find without having to pull everything off the shelf on your head first, and

Movable wire basket units provide extremely flexible toy storage. It is easy to see exactly what is inside without having to rummage, and the baskets can be interchanged to suit every situation. They also make tidying up a lot faster and less frustrating.

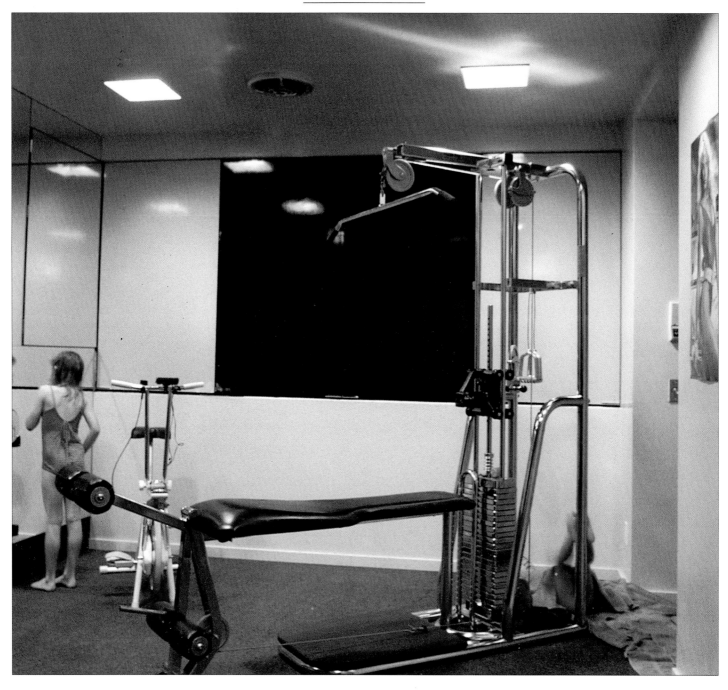

A basement family room can house the multi-gym and in this case has a sauna and jacuzzi adjoining. The floor to ceiling mirrors disguise large cupboards which house all the equipment and family games.

be equally (perhaps more importantly) easy to put away tidily. There are lots of specific storage ideas in the section on Children's Rooms (see p.84). Toys that are not often used but can't be thrown away yet should be stored high up, and games that are used by the whole family can be kept here too.

The room needs to change as your children grow. It's a good idea to let the children have their own television here so that you don't always have to watch the same cartoon video over and over again. Provide somewhere comfortable for the children to sit and watch with space for at least two other people to watch in equal comfort, or there will be arguments.

Each child in the family needs to have space to store their things. If you have a large age gap the older child may find a younger marauding child very difficult to deal with, so the older sibling's possessions should be kept childproofed against the smaller child. Find a childproof latch that the older child can open without difficulty, as the key to a lock is easily lost.

A real playroom should be a place where messy games can be played, and paintings can be painted without anyone complaining about the drips. For this a low basin built into a unit with space on either side to put things on is very useful. The floor covering should be washable (see p.81).

BASEMENT FAMILY ROOM

If you have a good sized basement, like a lot of North American homes do, your family room problems are over. As long as it is dry and warm, which it will be if your central heating boiler is situated there, well lit with plenty of space left to play, what more can you ask for.

A clothes washing area can be partitioned off in one corner and any storage or workshop area should be confined within another childproofed area, as children will be in the basement unsupervised most of the time.

DECORATION The walls and ceiling should be painted in a vinyl silk (latex semigloss) finish and in a pale warm colour, as there is usually not very much light in a basement. What light there is can then reflect back off the walls giving the whole room an airier feeling. This is a good opportunity to do some stencilling or a special paint finish with your children's help and ideas. Keep some walls free for balls to be bounced against while another area can be covered in posters and paintings, as mentioned above.

Some people like to put up wood panelling in basement rooms, probably to cover rough, unplastered walls, but this is not a sensible option if the room is to be used by children as the surface will not withstand the normal wear and tear of children's play. Have the walls rendered and rough painted with an exterior wall paint instead.

LIGHTING The ceiling is usually rather low, and for that reason hanging lights are not practical. The cheapest lights for this area are fluorescent tubes, but they can be hit by a stray football and they don't create a good atmosphere, as the light is rather cold. The best solution is recessed lights, hidden up in the ceiling. Get advice as to how many you need and where to put them when you buy them – a specialist retailer is best for this – because if this space is to be well lit you will probably need twice the number of fittings you have already. Have separate switches on dimmers for each corner, so that you don't have to light the whole area all the time. The dimmer switches will help create the right atmosphere when your teenage children want to impress their friends. You can use wall sconces if the basement doesn't get used for ball games.

FLOORING The floor is usually concrete and this is very good for most things except falling on your head, so a good investment for very active children might be plastic-covered gymnastic mats – they only have to be about 1in (25mm) thick. These can be stored on their sides against the wall, when they are not being used, in a very simply constructed rack.

FURNITURE There will need to be some comfortable seating on which to watch television, read, listen to music or talk to friends. A pool table and other large games can be set

For city children and keep-fit addicts a pull-up bar fitted into the family room doorway is fun, and a punch bag suspended from the ceiling is a good way of getting rid of your frustrations after a hard day at school.

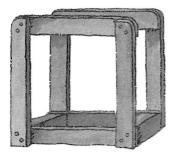

A simply constructed wooden holder for gymnastic mats or mattresses means they can be stored upright against a wall instead of in a space consuming heap.

RIGHT This ingenious small child's desk matches the chair, seen on the previous page. Again it is made by adapting vegetable racks, and, like the chair, can be raised by the addition of another rack on each side. A nice touch is the blue caterpillar task light.

RIGHT This upstairs playroom is very light, even on a dull day. The windows are made safe by clear rigid plastic sheets screwed firmly onto the window frames which are much more acceptable than prison-like bars and they do not exclude any light.

The long table means that three or four people can use it at once, and if this south-facing room gets too hot, the white Roman blinds can be pulled down, without losing much light. Hard-wearing carpet in a dirt-disguising colour has also been sprayed to guard against any spills.

up permanently, but while your children are small, try to keep a lot of space just to ride tricycles and run around in. If you have some central point, like the stairs from the upper floor, keep a wide clear path surrounding it for this kind of activity.

GAMES ROOMS

If your family is into large-scale indoor games like table tennis or pool, you will need space for the table, playing space around it, and storage for all of the equipment that goes with it. Badminton can also be set up to play indoors, but the room needs to be practically empty.

TABLE TENNIS TABLES These are all roughly the same size – 8ft x 4ft (244cm x 122cm) – and need about 4ft (122cm) clearance at either end to play in.

SNOOKER OR POOL TABLES These come in three sizes: 5ft x 2ft 6in (152cm x 76cm), 6ft x 3ft (183cm x 91cm) and

8ft x 4ft (244cm x 122cm). They need about 5ft (152cm) space all round the table to play in.

A wire mesh rack on the wall can store equipment like rackets, bats and balls, while snooker or pool cues can rest on wall hooks specially made for the purpose.

SOFT ROOM

A soft room is a wonderful resource for younger children from the age of two upwards. It could be converted into a games room as above as they grow out of the delight in throwing themselves about on foam cushions.

The more space in a soft room the better. Keep everything out of it unless it's soft and bouncy or is a platform to jump off. You need mats on the floor and wall, plastic-covered combustion modified fire-proofed foam mattresses and wedges, cushions, and maybe climbing ropes hanging from butchers' hooks screwed into the rafters or joists in the ceiling. Your children will find ways of using the equipment you wouldn't have thought possible.

It is a good idea to protect the windows (and your children) by fitting perspex (plexiglass) panels over the windows, and to pad any interior stud walls as the plasterboard or drywalls could be kicked in.

This is the ideal soft room, of course. Most of us have to compromise and use the room for other purposes as well. The

BELOW Chic but inexpensive, this adjustable wire shelving can be used to store all but the very smallest items.

RIGHT Intense concentration on the floor with a basket of Lego is a lot of children's idea of fun, but toys with small pieces can be a problem to store. Keeping them in a shallow close-weave basket has the advantage of making individual pieces much easier to find. This comfortable family room adjoins the kitchen on page 37. The family has adopted the traditional idea of masking the radiator behind a decorative guard which looks good and stops anyone from getting burnt. The large walk-in cupboard next to it has space at the bottom for drive-in toys, with adjustable shelves above. Quarry tiles are very easy to clean so are practical in a room that adjoins the garden, but they can be cold so a rug is needed to play on. This one has non-slip underfelt, particularly important where children are constantly running in and out.

spare room is the obvious choice, and you will have to decide whether your guests are going to sleep on a pile of mattresses or your children are going to use the spare bed to bounce on (see p. 126).

The best bounce next to a trampoline is an interior sprung (box spring) double bed. If you have an old one, your children will be thrilled if you can find a place to put it where they can enjoy it – they're less likely to be tempted to use yours instead. Bear in mind the ceiling below if it's above ground level. A barn or basement would be the best location.

If you don't have any spare space and would like to try to make a children's bedroom into a soft room you will need to keep everything else in tall cupboards with doors which close securely and cannot swing open against a bouncing child. Make sure that there are no sharp corners or extra furniture in the room that could be bounced into. If you're happy to do this and realize that the bed will have a limited life span, it is ideal to provide an interior sprung (box spring) bed with another mattress or truckle bed underneath for friends to both sleep and bounce on.

OVERLEAF A soft room like this is most children's dream, and adults' too, come to think of it. The permutations are endless; such a lot of energy can safely be expended in here, with such a lot of fun.

If you have an interior sprung bed that you can use for bouncing on remove the legs first, especially if they screw in, as they can't take the weight and break easily. Heavyweight hooks are screwed into the ceiling joists so they can take the weight of a swinging child and the windows are protected by a clear rigid plastic sheet with gaps for ventilation – very important as children get very hot after fifteen minutes' strenuous bouncing.

CHILDREN'S BEDROOMS

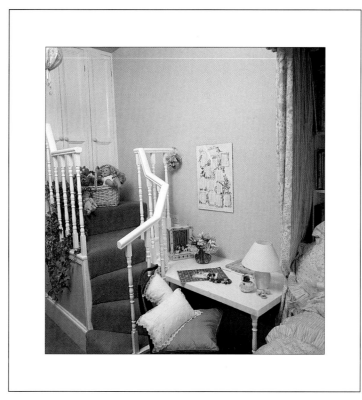

A child's bedroom is his or her home within your home, a personal haven, and it is the one place where you can allow your child's needs and preferences to take precedence over all others. Even when they have grown up and left home, many young adults still expect to return to 'their' room in the family home on weekend visits!

Even if you have a separate playroom, you will find as your children get older that they like to withdraw to the privacy of their own bedrooms, especially if there are other siblings, so there is bound to be a certain amount of crossover between bedroom and playroom. Where there is no separate playroom the bedroom is used more and more for play, so it needs to be carefully organized to provide maximum playing space. If two of your children have been sharing a room and are given the option of separate bedrooms, you may find that if they get on they prefer to remain sleeping in the same room and have the other as a playroom or sitting room, probably with their own television. If living space elsewhere in the home is at a premium, this may be a way of avoiding the living room being taken over by the children.

When you have a young baby who still wakes regularly at night for feeds and nappy changes, a small, cosy nursery close to the parents' bedroom is sensible, but it is better to move your children further away as they grow up. If your child's bedroom is also the playroom, let her have one of the largest bedrooms in the home, and use a smaller room to sleep in yourselves (see p. 104).

SHARING A ROOM

For two children sharing, bunk beds provide the most space-saving solution. Bunks like this with safety rails on both sides of the top bunk mean that the bunks do not have to be pushed against the wall, and each bunk has its own wall-mounted light-source. A long built-in desk and storage unit provides plenty of space for both children, and one or two friends. The dormer window in this attic room lets in natural light while being high enough to discourage climbing out.

If your children share a bedroom, it is usually because you don't have very much space, not because they choose to. The important consideration is to allow each child an individual area which can be defended from encroachments from the other side. Bunkbeds save precious floor space; the older child will have to be on the top bunk for the first six years of the younger one's life (see below). You may find that at that age the older child is quite happy to change over – many children enjoy the snug security of the bottom bunk.

Keep some storage that is completely out of reach or childproofed against the younger child, so the older child can keep precious things away from inquisitive and destructive little fingers. In return your older child should be asked to look out for anything that might be dangerous to the smaller child.

Twins require specially careful demarcation. Although identical twins often like to do everything together, it is worth gently prising them apart and trying to encourage the

<u>DECORATION</u> If you want to use a pretty wallpaper designed especially for babies but feel that it may be grown out of all too soon, remember that the room will probably need redecorating anyway when your child is four or five, so you can let your imagination go to town, and simply redecorate when it gets drawn on or outgrown. There are lots of wallpapers on the market that are fresh and pretty, not depicting a favourite TV character of the moment, that with the addition of a border designed for a baby's room can create a perfect atmosphere for a baby to enjoy going to sleep in. The border can be replaced when the baby is older, or the room may need to be used for a new baby anyway. An alternative is to paint the walls in a washable paint.

The choice of colour is not easy, especially if you are expecting a baby and don't know the sex. If you find deciding on a colour very difficult, and a lot of people do, use a fairly neutral pastel colour and let the toys, curtains and bedcovers add the colour accents.

Since the mid-seventies lead is not supposed to be used in paint, but you should always check with the retailer.

If you make a nursery out of a room that you have been using for another purpose and you don't want to redecorate completely, adding a frieze may be all you need to make it into a room ready for a new baby.

This personalized frieze has dates, photos and mementoes as well as a height chart which can be added to as the occupant of the room grows.

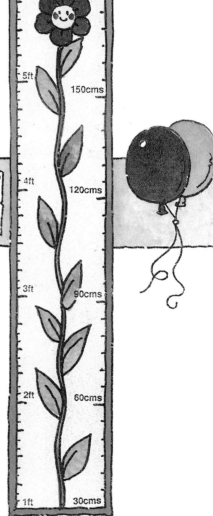

<u>TOYS</u> New babies are often given attractive soft toys and mobiles as presents. Because they don't actually play properly with soft toys until they are a few months old, it is a good idea to display them on a shelf where they can be seen but not reached.

Mobiles have a positive benefit in giving small babies something fascinating not only to look at but also, if they chime, something to listen to. They look very attractive strung across a nursery on fishing line: the more the better, especially in a small room. Unless they are specifically designed for hanging in the cot or crib, only hang mobiles from the ceiling – otherwise they will go straight into the baby's mouth. Most mobiles are made strictly to be looked at, not eaten, so you might be given one with toxic substances or made with wire attachments. You should also make sure that you don't hang them so they get entangled in your hair every time you come into the room. The strings of the mobile itself should be no more than 12in (30cm) to avoid entanglement.

<u>HEATING</u> The temperature in the nursery for a new baby should be around 70°F (21°C), so additional heating may be necessary, although it can be reduced after the first couple of months to a minimum of 60°F (15°C). An electric radiator to back up normal central heating is the best answer as it can be removed when the baby is bigger and stronger. On no account use any kind of heater with a naked flame or element.

A new cot or crib is a major outlay, but this model has been cunningly designed to convert first into a child's bed, and then into a comfy sofa for the playroom.

THE CRADLE OR BASSINETTE For the first three months, babies like to be enclosed and secure in something which is cosy and above all portable. A Moses basket or bassinette is light and easily available and can be lined prettily at home. However Moses baskets are not usually rigid enough for use in the car where you should use a proper carrycot fixed with restrainer straps.

COTS AND CRIBS Cots come in two main sizes: the regular – 48in x 23 in (123cm x 60cm), and the cot bed – 56in x 30in (144cm x 76cm). The latter is obviously more expensive but is good for large babies and it lasts longer as the sides can be taken off and replaced with a bed guard.

Whether you buy a cot new or second-hand, there are various safety points you should look out for. Don't buy a second-hand cot made before 1974 unless it is unpainted wood, as the original paint may have contained lead.

The corner posts of the cot should not be more than ⅝in (15mm) above the rest of the cot to prevent a baby's clothing becoming hooked onto it. There should be no vertical bars missing and they should not be more than 2 ⅜in (6cm) apart, that is the width of about four fingers, so that a baby's head cannot get stuck between them. Avoid cutouts in the head or foot boards as the baby's head might get stuck in them.

There should be two latches on a drop sided cot, one at each end, to make it very difficult for a toddler or small older child to open and get the baby out without your knowledge. If the cot is second-hand make sure you can replace these catches if they were to get broken. Check that the catches are easy to manipulate because you will use them a lot.

The cot mattress should fit closely with less than two fingers' space between mattress and cot bars, again to prevent your baby rolling into the gap and getting stuck. Even if you buy a second-hand cot, get a new mattress. If it is foam-filled, make sure it is combustion modified – this should be clearly labelled in the store. An interior sprung mattress gives a better bounce for an energetic toddler. Whatever the filling, a cot mattress should have one side covered with fabric and the other with PVC. While you are using the PVC side place a cotton undersheet or something washable between the mattress and the sheet to prevent your baby getting too hot and sweaty.

Some cots have different height settings for the mattress base. This is useful because when your baby is very small it is easier to get her out if the base is set at the highest level. When your baby can sit up put the mattress down to its lowest level. It won't be long before she starts to pull herself up, so you need to make climbing out very difficult.

Once a toddler shows signs of being able to climb out of the cot (and they usually do this by succeeding and landing with a bump on the floor, with obvious audible results), that is the time to switch to a bed with a bed guard, take the sides off a cot bed, or even lay a mattress on the floor. If you take this latter course, you cannot just make do with the cot mattress because your child will roll off it. As he will be able to move about freely, make sure that he can't hurt himself on anything low enough to reach and that all electric sockets are out of reach or sealed with socket guards. For safety you will either have to keep the door shut and use an intercom, or bar the entrance with an adjustable stair gate.

If your's is one of the children who doesn't try to climb out, and you have to make the decision about moving into a bed, the time to do this, with your child's agreement, is when her hands hit the bars at the side of the cot when turning over. Length is not usually a problem, although standing height may be and you should move your toddler once he or she is 35in (90cm) tall.

COT BUMPERS These protect a baby's head from hitting the bars of the cot, and they can also act as draught excluders. They should be covered in fabric rather than plastic as this becomes brittle after a while. They should be attached in at least six places and the strings should be cut as short as possible to make sure that your baby does not choke on one if she sucks it.

A bumper should be removed from the cot as soon as your baby can pull herself up to standing so that it isn't used as a convenient step when scaling the side of the cot.

A baby changing station which has been specially built to be the right height for the parent who uses it most. While it has its own running water supply, the taps are out of reach of a very small child but will later be very useful for an older child as well as for changing the baby. The guard rail which stops the baby from rolling off can easily be removed when the baby is toilet trained so the whole thing could be turned into a dressing table for an older child. The lid of the rubbish bin opens as you open the cupboard door so you only need one hand; change the rubbish bag daily.

CHANGING NAPPIES If you count up the number of times that you change a nappy a day and multiply it by how long your child is going to wear a nappy, you will see the importance of establishing a permanent changing station. Some people prefer to set this up in the nearest bathroom (see p 121) but if you want it in the nursery, make sure that the changing mat is placed on a firm surface at a comfortable height for you. Storage for all the things you use needs to be within easy reach, so that you don't have to leave the baby for a moment – because it's in that moment that your baby will decide to roll over and fall off onto the floor.

If you have a hand basin fitted (see the previous page) have it built into a unit incorporating an extended counter to use as a changing table, with cupboards underneath in which to place bins for soiled nappies, preferably fixed inside the cupboard door as in a kitchen. This unit could be removed or adapted later into a dressing table if the nursery goes on to become the child's permanent bedroom.

A table or desk that will be used later by your child is usually too low for an adult to change a nappy on. It's safer to use a changing table that has a guard rail around it and the storage will probably be more suited to a baby's needs.

A YOUNGER CHILD'S BEDROOM

The nursery decoration may not need to change as your child grows, especially during the pre-school years. The addition of cork tiles or a bulletin board made of soft board covered in felt will be useful for displaying paintings, photographs, badges and buttons, and so on.

During these years a younger sibling may have joined the family so it might be time for the older child to move on to a bigger and better room. This needs to be handled with great care so that the first child sees it as a part of being more grown up rather than feeling displaced by the new baby. The new room needs to have some feature that is much sought after, like a real desk, a full-length mirror or bed linen depicting the latest cartoon character favourite.

CURTAINS Most young children find it difficult to go to sleep when it is still light outside, and wake up with the birds at dawn. This can be partly overcome by providing curtains which are interlined with a dark coloured fabric, or, even better, fitting a dark blind behind the curtains. A metallic Venetian blind might appeal to high tech off-spring.

As your children get older not only are they reluctant to go to bed, but also may be difficult to get out of bed in the morning, especially on a school day. If this starts to happen, leave the blind up to let the light in through the curtains, which should help a bit. When you are buying fabric for curtains or blinds, remember that the light filtering through it will colour the room and it could be rather depressing to wake up in, say, bottle green gloom.

BEDROOMS FOR OLDER CHILDREN

An older child's bedroom needs to be decorated more like the bedroom of an adult with only a small hint of childhood, a teddy or two or a model aeroplane that has been built with a great deal of care. Posters of the current favourite pop stars

This bed complements the desk on page 93. The post-modern feel to the furniture in this teenage bedroom gives it style and is a very practical use of limited space. Some of the display shelves are behind glass so don't get too dusty and there is a cupboard at the end of the bed as well as drawers under it.

often entirely cover the walls so decoration doesn't need to be elaborate but it still needs to be washable. Have a care with all wall surfaces however – sticky tape lifts the surface off any wall covering, and even blue tac can adhere stubbornly when it has been up for a while and leaves a greasy mark. The least damaging is the good old drawing pin (thumb tack), but better still is a really large bulletin board or cork tiles covering a large area of wall.

A clothes basket should be within easy reach so there is no excuse for the dirty clothes to be left in a pile on the floor, or hidden under the bed.

By now your children will probably have strong ideas about what their room should look like or not be interested at all. If it's the former, don't be too ready to condemn the desire for black walls and metallic silver curtains or whatever. After all, if it's what he wants he's the one who is going to live with it.

At the point when you'd rather not know what time your teenage or young adult children get in at night, it may be worth moving the bedrooms around so that theirs are as far away from yours as possible. They will feel less restricted and you won't be woken up by heavy footfalls at three in the morning or by the music that plays a large part in most teenagers' lives. As effective sound proofing is expensive, this move – plus a good quality personal stereo – may save you years of nagging. On the other hand, if you would rather be able to hear that reassuring turn of the key in the lock, then make sure your bedroom is within earshot.

BELOW It is sometimes difficult to know how to provide a teenage boy with a stylish bedroom which he is also going to accept. This split-level arrangement is one very good answer – storage is built in under the platform and half a wall is given over to a cork bulletin board with enough room for the latest and greatest poster favourites. Dancing on the raised platform may cut down a bit on the headache factor for those living below.

RIGHT This teenager's bedroom has a canopy over the bed supported by photographic poles. The fairy lights give the bed a magical quality; they are quite safe as they don't get hot and the material is flame resistant.
The task light in the desk gives ample light to work by while retaining the atmosphere.

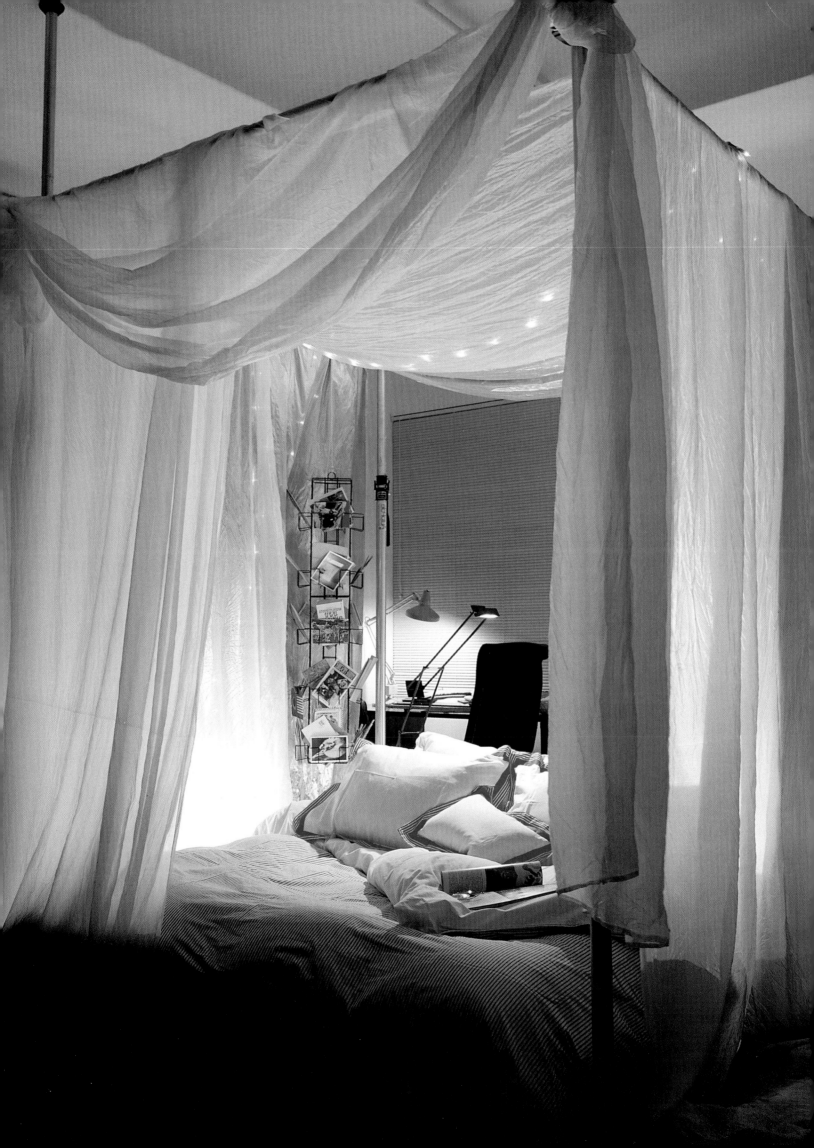

PARENTS' BEDROOMS

ABOVE The perfect place to spend a summer evening when your teenage children are cooking supper for friends downstairs, the end of this large bedroom is used for getting away from the television, for writing and relaxing. A parents' bedroom need not just contain a bed and wardrobe, but can also be furnished with comfortable easy chairs and chaises longues, upholstered in the sort of colours you'd never dare use in the child-orientated areas of the house. The window leads onto a balcony overlooking the garden, so it has a child lock on it, as does the window behind the window seat.

While your children are very small there usually isn't much time to spend in your own bedroom, apart from dropping into bed at the end of the day. Most parents remember the nights when they could have slept in a barn, just as long as they were left to sleep for four hours at a stretch. So at least for the first few years of parenthood, the important point about the parents' bedroom is that the bed is easy to make and the room itself easy to keep clean and tidy. The layout of your home will dictate the positioning of your bedroom in relationship to your children's rooms. You should be close enough to enable you to hear them if they need you, but this doesn't mean that they have to be next door except when they are babies.

As the children grow older, you may use your bedroom as a haven of peace away from the rest of the family, or just a quiet place to go and work out what to say to the teacher about little Alice's problem with quadratic equations. Once your children reach their teens, the bigger the distance between theirs and your bedroom the better – preferably with their room below yours, so that you aren't disturbed by noise late into the night, and they have more freedom too.

If space is a problem, as it often is with a growing family, the master bedroom – often one of the largest rooms in the house – may be better used as a bedroom/playroom for the children, or even a family room, so that the living room can be used simply for sitting in rather than for wall-to-wall Lego. With careful storage design, a smaller bedroom can easily fulfil the needs of two busy parents who may hardly use it.

If the room is too small for a good-sized bed and storage space for two sets of clothes, think about using a dressing room. It doesn't have to be near your own room if it is simply

RIGHT The parents in this family have opted for a small bedroom at the top of the house and have given over the master bedroom to be used as a bedroom/playroom by the children, although this has not prevented determined encroachment! Every available space is used for storage in order to make the room work for two people.

The mirror-door cupboards for hanging clothes are complemented by another shallower cupboard on the left side of the window with drawers and shelves for more clothes and accessories. Because the Victorian bedstead is so high off the floor there is plenty of space underneath for white wire baskets containing items like shoes, which are usually disguised by a long valance that matches the curtains.

going to be somewhere to keep your clothes. And it doesn't have to be very large – a good sized walk-in closet is quite adequate and could be built into an under-used space such as a large landing.

Don't feel you have to be locked into a bedroom design for the rest of your life. The only rule here is to be comfortable in what works best for you at the time; change it if its use is outgrown. For instance, when the children are approaching their teens, it might be time for you to take over a larger bedroom in which you can comfortably sit and watch television or read, as well as sleep, on the nights when your teenage children have friends round. If you can retire gracefully to your bedroom to do the things you want to do without feeling resentful, they can entertain their friends without having you around to cramp their style.

BEDS

Since their sleep is so often broken, parents deserve to sleep in a decent bed. When you are choosing a bed, there are family factors to take into account as well as the usual practical considerations like whether the mattress is hard or soft enough, or whether you can get the bed up the stairs. For instance, if your room is small would it be a good idea to buy a bed with storage capacity underneath or just space enough to keep the golf clubs? Is there space for a really wide bed so that when the children spreadeagle themselves in the middle of it rather too early in the morning, you have a bit more at the edges on which to snatch those extra minutes of sleep?

STORAGE

If you go for the option of taking a smaller room then use every available space. Things stored under the bed should be as easy to get at as possible so that you don't need to scrabble right underneath to get them out. It would also be thoughtful to leave a child-sized space for hide-and-seek if your children haven't grown out of it. Shelves or cupboards above the bed can be used for storing things you don't use every day.

Any medicines or personal items that are kept in the bedroom should be securely locked away, inside the wardrobe (see p.121). Even a nail file could cause severe damage. A child may wander into your bedroom alone while looking for you, or fetching something, or searching for birthday presents a week in advance, so keeping dangerous or valuable items out of reach is not enough, especially when the children are small.

How you store your clothes is up to you – the idea of a dressing room has already been discussed, but in a small room remember that a chest of drawers takes up potentially more space than a cupboard with shelves. Make sure your wardrobe is stable and that a child couldn't get locked inside.

If there is another bathroom for the rest of the family, then an en suite or master bathroom is ideal, especially if you have live-in help (see p.123). Depending on its size, the bathroom can provide useful storage space as well.

THE BEDROOM AS A WORKROOM

Your bedroom can be used very well as a workroom as it is unused during the day and most of the evening. You have the

The corner of this bedroom provides a quiet space, cleverly designed not to clash with the overall look of the room, to write and keep household documents out of the reach of small fingers.
The antique office cabinet behind the desk means that everything from sewing kits to school reports, from electricity bills to notes for the new novel can be kept neatly organized with no danger of unsightly piles on the desk top collecting the dust.

advantage of being able to shut the door on it if you have to stop work in the middle of something to attend to a crisis or make the supper. Small fingers are less likely to re-arrange your work than if you are doing it on the kitchen or dining room table and you are less likely to find a piece of bread and jam filed under 'O' some weeks later. If your bedroom is a long way from where the children usually play and you're working while they are at home it is helpful to instal an intercom so that you can communicate with each other without the frustration of shouting from opposite ends of the house. The only people who can hear what's being said properly in this situation are the neighbours, and meanwhile disaster can strike because the children thought you said 'yes' when in fact you had been yelling 'no' at the top of your voice.

ELECTRIC APPLIANCES AND SAFETY

It is useful to have a double electric socket either side of the bed for the intercom, bedside lights, radio etc, and at least one other double socket conveniently situated near a mirror. If you are using the bedroom to work in you will need more than three double sockets. If you use an electric blanket or have any kind of fire in the room instal a smoke alarm on the ceiling (see p.15). Before you go to bed at night check that the way to your children's bedroom is clear of obstructions, especially if you sleep on different floors.

LEFT Using the bright primary colours usually associated with children is unusual in a bathroom, but it is stunningly effective in this large family bathroom. As it is mainly used by children, the two basins side by side help to avoid arguments and the bath toys are kept in plastic toy boxes under them.

The 6in (15cm) wide space surrounding the bath is useful for resting bath toys on in the middle of a game, and makes it safer when getting small children out of the bath, and the simple idea of continuing the flooring up the side of the bath makes it easy to clean and a satisfyingly solid shape.

Babies and children generally like to spend a lot of time playing in the bath, so the bathroom should be a warm, inviting room where you also enjoy spending time. In fact, it often becomes a relaxing place where the family congregates for a chat at the end of the day. If you have the space, the addition of a comfortable chair means that you don't have to spend hours perched on the toilet seat singing nursery rhymes or testing your children's knowledge of the times table.

A family home should preferably have two bathrooms or a bathroom and a shower room. Once they have grown out of the stage of not washing at all, older children especially occupy bathroom space for more time than seems possible, so one bathroom tends to lead to family friction. If this isn't possible, there should at least be two toilets, and it is helpful to have one near the kitchen to reduce the risk of 'accidents' when your children are young. The floor covering round the toilet bowl must clean easily, whether there are boys in your family or not. Even if your children are all girls there are bound to be boys around, especially when they are teenagers.

Babies and toddlers require a certain amount of equipment in the bathroom. Unless you have a changing table set up in the nursery, you will probably have a changing mat in the bathroom, plus the baby's changing gear, and later, a potty, a child's toilet seat and a step stool. If your bathroom is upstairs, it makes life easier to have two sets of equipment, one kept in the downstairs toilet. If your children are close together in age, you may find you're using all of this equipment at the same time, so try to keep it off the floor, because it looks untidy and could be trodden on or tripped over.

ABOVE The well-lit mirrors in this bathroom, which leads off a parents' bedroom, are also cupboards for toiletries, but not medicines as it doesn't lock. Because the mirror doors open they can be positioned to show the side of your face, which often needs constant scrutiny when you are a teenager.

The most obvious answer is a vanity unit (see below), but remember it is dangerous to keep any toxic cleaners or toiletries in there at the same time. Many downstairs toilets are very small and leave no space for a vanity unit, so hang a travelling changing kit on the back of the door instead, and tuck the potty and the stepping stool behind the toilet.

DECORATION

Because there is a lot of condensation in a bathroom, especially a small one, a vinyl silk or semigloss paint gives the longest lasting and easy-to-clean finish. Damp air can lift the edges of wallpaper, especially round the bath, and it soon starts to peel and look shabby, so should be avoided.

Tiles are very resilient, and are best for a splashback for the bath and hand basin, and inside a shower. A border tile helps

Because this landing is above the kitchen it was the perfect place to add a small extra bathroom as the water supply is nearby, and in order not to lose the light the windows and the door leading to it are made of frosted glass.

RIGHT Bathrooms need not be cold and clinical, they can like this one be made into comfortable rooms where people feel able to sit and relax. The window seat is positioned over a radiator with child-locked casement windows behind, and the comfortable chair would make any family conference difficult to end. Antique fittings like the Victorian toilet bowl and basin (fitted with modern plumbing) go well with the heavily-varnished floor and the free-standing Edwardian bath which allows plenty of room for manoeuvre when bathing small children.

to get rid of the municipal feeling that tiles can produce. However, tile design has really taken off in recent years and there are many attractive shapes and colourways to choose from.

Tongue and groove boards can also make an unusual splashback and bath panelling. They need to be very well sealed with varnish or paint, which needs renewing regularly. Wood is not quite as easy to clean as tiles, but does look very attractive.

FLOORING

The most important thing about the floor in your bathroom is that it should not be slippery when wet. It should not show the dirt, either: if you walk on a wet floor in shoes any dirt on the soles leaves a mark. Vinyl sheeting is probably the most practical flooring, although stripped and sanded floor boards that have been really well sealed with marine varnish are also effective in a bathroom, so long as the cracks have been filled

LEFT Although the children have their own bathroom in this household, they still sometimes like to use this one which leads off their parents' bedroom. A large bath mat is an essential item to protect the carpet from splashing and cupboards at each end of the bath conceal a few bath toys which have wandered from their proper home. The radiator under the window is also a heated towel rail, while the large basin has been set into an old-fashioned wash stand.

On the left-hand wall a specially-built shower unit has been incorporated; as shown below.

BELOW The elevation shows the left wall of the bathroom opposite. The vanity unit is placed centrally against a false wall which hides a shower with a seat, to the left of the basin; the toilet and bidet are on the right. Both of these cubicles have an extractor fan and light. The opaque glass in the doors lets in light without reducing privacy.

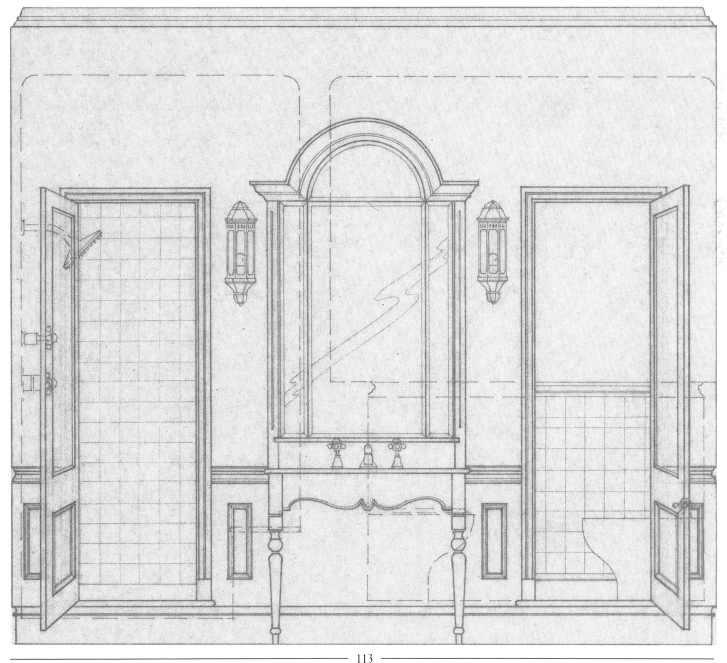

with wooden fillets to keep out draughts. Look for floor coverings which are designed to be slip-proof; non-slip marble or unglazed ceramic floor tiles are easy to clean and particularly good for a shower room. Many homes with this sort of flooring have a drain fitted into the floor to remove excess surface water.

Vinyl or cork tiles tend to lift at the edges if they get wet often and for that reason are not really suitable for a bathroom that is used a lot by children. Carpet is not very practical either, even if it is washable, especially if your children are boys. However it does give the room a cosy warm feel and you may want to use it. If so, there are a few ways to overcome the problems it presents; simply use a very big bath mat or instal a low uncarpeted wooden platform, about 3in (7.5cm) above floor level and 3ft (93cm) wide, running the whole length of the bath. Covered with tiles or vinyl, this looks interesting and provides a good space for everyone to dry themselves on.

LIGHTING

A bathroom needs general light, probably from the ceiling, a fitting in the shower, if relevant, and fittings that light your face around the mirror. These should not be pointed at the mirror, lighting it instead of you, because you will find that you have to put your nose right up to the glass to light your face. Don't be afraid of too much light – a mirror that is properly lit with warm, incandescent strip lights around it is much more flattering and less frustrating than a badly-lit one. Fluorescent light is too cold in a bathroom.

BATHROOM FURNISHINGS

BATHTUBS If you are installing a bathtub that you will want to use for the children don't buy one that is too large. A large tub uses a lot of water even for a shallow bath, and it is difficult to reach down to your children to wash them if it is too deep. A bath that is sunk into the floor would be uncomfortable for the same reason. A step running the length of the bath makes it easier for children to get in and out. It needs to be 12in (30cm) wide so that you can kneel on it comfortably.

Unless you are a very tall family the most comfortable length for a bath is 5ft 3in (160cm). By the age of seven, most children can lie down in it without sliding down all the time. However, a bigger bath means that children can bath together for longer with fewer arguments about who has the most space and whose turn it is to be up the tap end. Taps positioned in the middle of the bath avoid this wrangle altogether. Even if your bath has a nonslip bottom it is wise to use an anti-slip mat once your baby starts to sit up independently.

The tiles around a bath should be at least 20in (52cm) high to catch the splashes and higher – 3ft (93cm) – if there is a

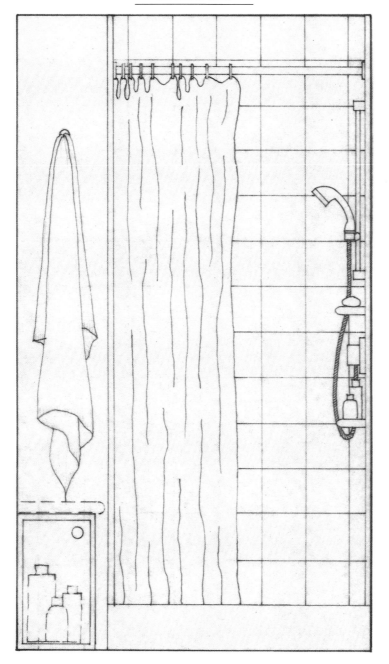

A shower designed with a family in mind, incorporating a number of features that make it easy for everyone to use it. The shower head slides up and down a metal pole so that children can reach it and the spray doesn't hit them from a great height. The shower controls are low enough for everyone to reach comfortably and there are two shelves providing ample space for the array of different shampoos, soaps and conditioners that a family seems to accumulate. The seat gives extra elbow room for growing fourteen year olds. As well as being a place for contemplation, it provides a small cupboard space for toiletries which opens from the outside of the shower.

shower attachment, which makes children's hair-washing sessions far easier. A shower curtain that completely encloses the bath enables your children to splash about without having too much mopping up to do afterwards.

If the taps are at the end of the bath, and the bath is against the wall, the cold tap should be on the outside edge, so that when your child decides that his favourite teddy must have a wash he doesn't burn himself with hot water or empty the hot water tank just when it's time for baby brother to have a bath. It isn't necessary to have your water boiling hot anyway – it saves energy and avoids scalds if you keep the thermostat at minimum or just above.

SHOWERS Your shower needs to be thermostatically controlled to ensure that if the cold water is turned on somewhere else in the house the person in the shower doesn't get scalded. It should also have an individual water pressure adjustment so that in similar circumstances someone having a shower isn't suddenly left with a miserable trickle.

This large room has been divided in half to make a bedroom and an en suite bathroom. The bathroom includes a cleverly designed shower/bath ideal for children's use. The shower curtain can surround the whole bath to allow maximum splashy play, and the shower can be hand held for hair washing.

Small children find showers rather frightening at first, but when they are older showering is a very economical and quick way to get clean. If you have the opportunity to put in a shower build one in rather than buying a ready-made cubicle, so that it is custom-made for your family's needs. A seat is a good idea, plus lots of places to put all the different shampoos and other paraphernalia that each member of the family tends to accumulate.

BABY BATHS It isn't really necessary to have a separate baby bath – the length of time a baby is small enough to use one is rarely more than four months, and you could equally well use a large sink with facecloths tied round the taps, or a large washing up bowl – you can even buy specially shaped foam pads that fit into an ordinary bath and on which the baby lies. However, many parents prefer to bath their babies in a purpose-made baby bath because it is smaller and at a convenient height. A baby bath can be used in the nursery, instead of the bathroom, which might be better if it is warmer and all the baby's equipment is kept there. The temperature of the room when bathing a baby should be 80°F (27°C).

If you are going to buy a baby bath, think about where you are going to keep it and make sure it has a plug to drain the water into a bucket, as a full baby bath is extremely heavy and awkward to empty. Baby baths are inevitably bulky so find one that you can hang up over the bathtub, with a folding stand that can be tucked away. There are baths which can be fitted over the full-size tub resting on the sides, and you can even buy changing tables which incorporate a bath. As with most modern baby equipment, there is plenty of ingenious choice, so it is worth shopping around to find what suits you best.

HAND BASINS In the bathroom used most often by the children you may feel able to have the basin fitted at a height of about 30in (76cm). This is 6in (15cm) lower than usual, but young children can easily reach it, reducing the time that a stepping stool is needed, and making it easier to reinforce the habit of hand-washing after using the toilet. A low basin is only inconvenient for adults over six feet tall, and it will be your children and their friends who use it most often. If you only have one bathroom or you don't want to go to the trouble of lowering the hand basin, a bidet is an unusual but surprisingly effective alternative (see below).

A single-handled faucet or 'Unitap' really makes washing easier for children. They soon get used to keeping the control in the right place so that the water comes out at a comfortable temperature. If you have conventional taps check that they are easy to turn on and off and that they are clearly colour-coded hot (red) and cold (blue).

If you have the room, two basins side by side make it easier for more than one child to wash or clean teeth at the same time without one getting an elbow in another's ear, with inevitable consequences. Even if you only have one basin, there should be plenty of room on either side.

MIRRORS As adults hang mirrors over basins they usually position them at the right height for themselves, which is of course hopeless for children. It has been proved that children clean their teeth better if they can see themselves in a mirror. A large mirror that comes down to the level of a 6in (15cm)

A simple vanity unit relying on the enamelled taps and door knobs for colour accents. The cupboard is surprisingly spacious, holding all the toiletries, a step stool and the bath toys, which are kept in a plastic basket to allow air to circulate so they don't get musty. The doors are fitted with childproof locks. Because the splash back stops the mirror being any lower two self adhesive mirror tiles are used to make sure the children can see themselves to clean their teeth. The tiles can be removed using lighter fuel when the children have grown.

tile splash-back suits all but the smallest children. Until they are tall enough to see themselves in it, stick a mirror tile onto the splash-back at child height with double-sided sticky pads so that it can be removed easily when the children are taller, or buy tiles with sticky backs.

TOWELS AND TOWEL RAILS Towels need to be hung at a height where your children can reach them easily and put them back, so they have no excuse for leaving them in a heap. A heated towel rail should be attached to the hot water system rather than the central heating system so that the rail will still be hot when the heating is off. Electrically heated towel rails have to be safely wired in. Any heated towel rail should be large enough to accommodate enough towels for the whole family. Bear in mind that it could become hot enough to burn a young child's sensitive skin so always keep a towel on it when the children are in the bathroom.

If each member of the family has their own colour towels and face cloths or sponges, there is less risk of passing on infections. Many people like to have matching bathroom linen, which echoes the bathroom decoration. If you like this idea, lighter and darker tones of the same colour can work just as well to differentiate family members' towels and face cloths. If you use this personalized system there are also fewer arguments about whose towel is the dry one hanging up and whose is the one in a dank heap left over from a game under the hose in the garden.

TOILETS There could be a time when you need to buy a lock for the toilet seat. This may seem ridiculous, but things do get stuffed down the toilet, requiring the services of an emergency plumber, or you could find yourself watching your rather nice new earrings being flushed away before you had a chance to wear them. Worst of all, lack of a toilet lock might result in the handing round to little friends of tiny tea cups full of water taken from the toilet because it is at an accessible height.

While the children are small it is safer not to use bleach-based flush fresheners in the cistern just in case a child drinks the water. You may feel that your child would never be so stupid, and you are probably right, but children do goad each other on sometimes.

Top flushing cisterns are not easy for young children to use, and they will leap at any excuse not to flush the toilet. If you already have this type of cistern, consider having it changed to a conventional lever handle.

BIDETS When you are recovering from a birth, a bidet is seventh heaven. However, the taps are accessible to very young children so they need to be firmly turned off. The type

A basement is a perfect place to instal a family bath or spa. Because they hold a lot of water they are very heavy and would need strong joists in an upper room to hold them and a large water tank. This spa is completely surrounded by tesselated tiles so that any splashing doesn't matter, and the room provides a place for water play during winter months.

which provides a jet of water is particularly tempting as children love the idea of an indoor fountain, but unsupervised experimentation could cause a flood.

On the other hand, the low level of a bidet provides unlooked-for benefits to the parents of very small children. If you choose a non-fountain type with a unitap and decide from the start for hygiene reasons that you are going to give it over exclusively to your infant's use, it can become an ideal low level hand basin, either for a parent changing a baby on the floor or for a toddler learning to wash his own hands and face. It also provides a delightful miniature boating lake, allowing for endless supervised play while you snatch a shower or soak in the tub. You will have to alert your guests that the bidet is not for general use, of course.

<u>DOOR LOCKS</u>　A simple sliding lock is best, set at a height that a small child can't reach (see the height and reach chart on p.169). From the age of about six, your children may prefer to be able to lock the door so that other people can't come in when they are using the toilet. Locks that are specifically made for bathrooms can be opened from both sides of the door, although not easily from the outside. It is important to fit this sort of lock as a child panics very easily if he thinks he is locked in and has visions of being shut in the bathroom for ever, living on omelettes posted under the door. To avoid this trauma when you are out, teach your children how to lock other bathroom and toilet doors, as well as your own.

In addition to a lock on the inside, you may need a bolt on the outside of the door that keeps small children out, for their own safety. If you have older children, position this outer bolt low enough for them to reach it and write a reminder on the door to lock it after they have left the bathroom.

STORAGE

There is a lot to store in a bathroom and a vanity unit built round the hand basin comes in very useful for bath toys and bulky items like toilet paper. If you have two basins side by side the storage space is doubled. With children under six in the house, you should childproof this cupboard space if you need to keep toxic or dangerous items in it – remember that this includes seemingly innocuous cosmetics like shampoo and skin cream. Apart from the safety aspect, expensive after-shave, pink hair conditioner and green bubble bath make tempting ingredients for a delightful concoction mixed in the basin with the business end of daddy's toothbrush. So unless you're very tolerant and prepared to keep an eye on this sort of experimentation, lock your bathroom toiletries away.

A built-in cupboard at one or both ends of the bath gives it a lovely enclosed feeling and lots of space that could be used for dirty linen, bath toys, or, if properly childproofed, for bathroom cleaners and the toilet brush. A bath that is enclosed with panels should have one removable panel to allow access to plumbing – this could also be used for storing such items as potties and children's toilet seats when not in use. If storage space is in very short supply, don't scorn the old-fashioned bathroom stool that has space in it for storage.

Keep the bath toys in a cupboard, in small, open-sided plastic baskets. If the toys become cloudy with scum clean them by soaking them in warm water and washing-up liquid,

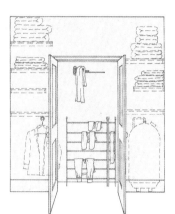

A walk-in airing cupboard designed for drying clothes as well as storing sheets and towels, this could equally well be built into a utility room or basement if there is a heat source such as a central heating boiler. It means that all the drying can take place behind closed doors and you need never see another pair of Levi 501s suspended over the living room radiator to dry 'because they'll shrink in the tumble drier'. All the shelves are slatted, which means that warm air can circulate easily. The lower shelves shown empty here are for drying clothes; they are not all the same depth to make it easier to reach to the back, and the slats are close together so that small socks don't fall through.
Shirts can be drip-dried and the clothes horse is removable. Long items like trousers, towels or sheets can be dried or aired hanging from the wall-mounted airer.

then scrubbing them with a nail brush. If you think the plastic is durable enough, you could put them in the dishwasher.

If your hot-water tank is situated in the bathroom (or even if it is not) and the room is big enough, it makes sense to have an airing cupboard built round it with slatted shelves to allow maximum circulation of warm air. If this can be made floor to ceiling than your storage problems are all solved, and it could be used as a drying cupboard too.

When your children are babies, a chest of drawers of the right height for changing on or a purpose-made changing table, can provide storage for all the baby's things. If it isn't near enough to the basin for you to reach while keeping a hand on your baby, always use a separate bowl of water kept near at hand while changing.

MEDICINE CABINETS A good childproof cabinet is very important to avoid possibly fatal accidents and for peace of mind. Some open from the side or have sliding doors, and may be mirrored. The safest type has a door that is latched at the top and hinges down to make a shelf to put the medicines on when they are being handed out. Fix the cabinet at about shoulder height for the shortest adult using it. If you keep a chair or stool in the bathroom, try to make it as difficult as possible for a child to use it to climb up to the medicine cabinet. There are also small locking cabinets available that can be fitted inside another cupboard. If you are in any way worried about how childproof your bathroom cabinet is, make sure it is too high for a small child to reach.

A brightly painted bathroom seat conceals a dirty clothes basket with a difference – it's time as well as space saving. There are four divisions and the children have been taught to separate their clothes all ready for washing, with whites in one, strong colours in another, towels in another, and so on.

LIVE-IN HELP

LEFT The perfect environment for an independently minded live-in helper, this room is at the top of the house, with stairs leading up to a small, high-sided roof garden cut out of the roof. The living and kitchen area has been designed with the teenagers who will subsequently use it in mind, and their safety while still small children in the care of a nanny. There is a separate room to sleep in and another bedroom on the same floor is used as the spare room so that guests can be free to use this kitchen should they want to.

Sometimes it's hard enough living with your own family, let alone a stranger who might not even speak the same language, so bringing someone into your home to help look after the children requires quite a lot of positive thinking. Although this isn't the place to go into the pros and cons of choosing a person to live in, what is relevant here is to think about how much you are going to assimilate this person into your family life, or whether you expect her to keep her life separate, apart from the time when she is actually working.

Live-in help can mean anything from a trained nanny to an au pair, but there are common denominators: the person is usually young and female. Her room, or rooms, in your home are also her home for the time being, and the more facilities you can provide for her the happier everyone will be. Any special alterations you make to these rooms at this time could be used by teenage children in the future, helping them to be more independent. Make the room as attractive as possible, with adequate storage not just for clothes but also for the possessions that will make your nanny or au pair feel at home, such as books and records or cassettes, photographs, plants and ornaments. Although few people can be expected to provide a hifi, a small television is a good idea.

Bathroom facilities of her own mean less pressure in the whole family, but may be difficult to instal if space is at a premium or plumbing is difficult. At the very least you should have two toilets in your home, and it is really better to have

ABOVE A nanny or au pair living in your home needs to feel that her privacy and comfort are being catered for. Anyone would be happy in this unusual and attractive conversion, where a low top floor ceiling has been removed to bring light and space. The addition of a bathroom behind the bed means that there is no pressure on bathrooms in other parts of the house, and a kitchen is built in behind the doors at the end of the passage.

This cupboard hides a well lit basin so that the rest of the room can feel like a bedsitting room rather than a bathroom when the cupboard door is closed.

two bathrooms so that there are no embarrassing confrontations first thing in the morning. If there is only one bathroom, consider installing a wash-basin in the nanny's room or find a small corner to instal a shower for the whole family's use. There is no reason why this should not be downstairs, if this is where you have the space.

A small kitchen for her own use means that she can eat when she wants to and you don't have to skirt round her in the evening trying to cook dinner for six guests after a hard day at work. With the advent of small portable ovens and grills and microwave ovens a compact kitchen is a more realistic alternative these days, provided there is adequate ventilation.

Bear in mind however that strictly speaking an au pair lives as one of the family and is expected to share the family's meals – a factor reflected in her wages, which are usually not much more than pocket money.

THE BED

Make sure that the bed is comfortable – if you have to use the bed passed on from Aunty Betty in 1969, at least buy a new mattress. No carer can be expected to be kind and creative to bumptious children at 8.30am after nights of discomfort on a lumpy old mattress.

If you decide on a sofa-bed, it needs to have proper interior springing as it's to be slept on every night. A futon is a good alternative as it doubles up as a sofa and looks smart. Another idea is to provide a truckle bed, which slides under an ordinary divan when not in use. This enables your nanny or au pair to have a friend to stay occasionally, or a new nanny can overlap with an out-going incumbent for a smooth handover.

Although loft beds on stilts are excellent space savers (see p.89), they probably aren't a good idea for your live-in help. Not everyone likes sleeping high up, and as the occupiers of the room will undoubtedly change from time to time it is better to be more conventional.

OTHER FURNITURE

A well-lit table is essential. It doesn't need to be very big but think about what it may be used for – perhaps studying, writing, eating, sewing or even putting on make-up. A table with drawers, or even a desk if your help always eats with the family, provides extra storage space. An adjustable work lamp provides a good flexible light source. There should be adequate seating for at least two people. Folding chairs that are high enough to use at the table are space-saving and may allow room for at least one other comfortable chair.

Provide a long mirror on the wall or cupboard. Make sure there is a lockable cabinet for any medicines and jewellery she may bring with her, both of which could be swallowed by young children. Instil in her how important it is to use it.

If you can afford it, instal a separate telephone line so that you aren't constantly taking messages or calling up the stairs. The quarterly bills will show exactly how much she has used the phone. It avoids later resentment on both sides if you can agree from the start what proportion of her bill you are prepared to pay. These negotiations will also prove to be helpful if your teenage children occupy the space later.

RIGHT There is almost a complete kitchen in this cupboard, which houses a sink, a two-ring stove top and an oven. The fridge is in another cupboard behind the door, along with the crockery. Combined with a small bathroom, a bedroom and the living/dining room in which this kitchenette is situated, a professional nanny can have complete independence from the rest of the family in her own small apartment at the top of the house.

SPARE ROOMS

ABOVE *What could be nicer than to be shown into this room after ten hours' travelling with two small children. Although the room is relatively small, there is plenty of space for clothes with a wall of cupboards to the left of the camera and drawers under the bed.*

It is very nice to have the space to accommodate house guests comfortably without having to turf other members of the family out of their rooms or have to use the sitting room sofa. Yet spare rooms are often given second-class status in the domestic pecking order, and can become soulless places simply from lack of use. One of the best ways of finding out whether the spare room is comfortable is to sleep in it yourself. A spare room is by definition for the use of adult guests – visiting children usually share rooms with your own children, as this is half the fun.

If your spare room is only used occasionally, you could adapt it for your children's use the rest of the time. A spare room doubles up particularly well as a 'soft room' (see p.74). This is a room where children can fool around without causing any damage – every home should have one. The bed needs to be strong enough to take the bouncing, flopping, leaping and somersaulting to which children will subject it, and this goes for the ceiling of the room below as well, if the spare room is not at ground level. A foam sofa-bed is good both for your guests to sleep on and for your children to hurl themselves onto when zapped by the Droids or whatever. (Make sure, of course, that the foam upholstery is made from combustion-modified, fire resistant foam – see p.15.)

The room decoration needs to take this double purpose into account, so a washable paint or wallpaper finish is fundamental. A good alternative to conventional decoration is to use one of the painting techniques such as rag rolling, marbling or sponging. As well as being decorative in their own right, these disguise fingerprints and can be varnished to make them easy to clean.

Keep this spare/soft room as empty of furniture as possible. Any extra cushions or thin mattress-shaped pieces of foam only required for bouncing should have their own storage

RIGHT *A spare room can double as a soft room when it's not occupied by guests. The uncluttered arrangement of this relaxed spare room means that it is easy to organize for both functions. The shelf flaps down when the cushions and children are flying and the things on the shelf go into the cupboard to the right of the camera.*

space under the bed or in a wardrobe or closet close by, so that they can disappear easily when you use the room for guests.

A workroom could also double as a spare room (though not as a soft room), as long as whatever work you do in that room can wait while your guests are in residence. You also need to be able to tidy it away satisfactorily to avoid inconveniencing them too much.

STORAGE

You don't need very much storage space in a spare room if it is only to be used for occasional visitors. A small cupboard with shelves and some hanging space left for their belongings is probably enough. All too often this space is used as an overflow for family detritus, so that instead of a fresh-smelling, newly-lined empty shelf or two, your guest is faced with a dusty old vacuum cleaner that hasn't worked for two years and those clothes handed on from cousin Tanya which your children grew into and out of without you even remembering they were there. Be ruthless about this sort of junk; get rid of it or find somewhere else to store it.

SAFETY

If your child is under five years old, it's wise to ask your guests to keep the door of their room shut during their stay. Fit a cover to the door knob (see p.13) to make sure your child cannot wander in and explore your guests' belongings, especially as there may be medications, breakables or valuables among them. Children need to learn to respect other people's privacy, but if they are young and have been accustomed to coming and going as they please in the spare room at other times, you cannot really blame them for forgetting that the room has other temporary occupants.

The drawing below shows how the brilliantly designed spare room opposite converts into a fully-fledged workshop (overleaf). The bed folds away when the room is used for carpentry, leaving a totally empty space in which to work safely.

The room has been divided to provide visitors with their own bathroom. The closet on the right holds all the bedding and there is space for all their clothes.

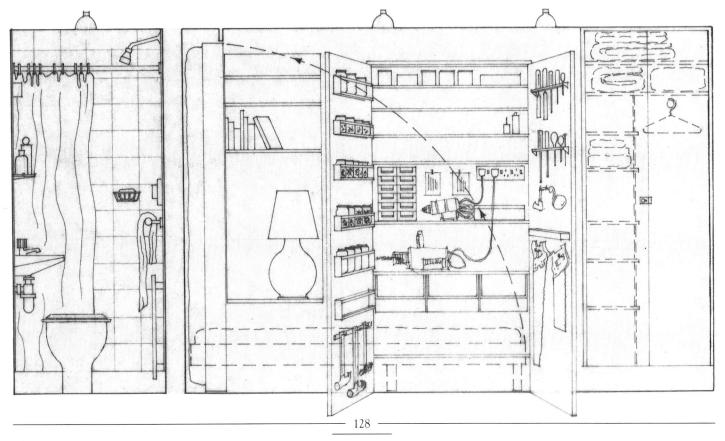

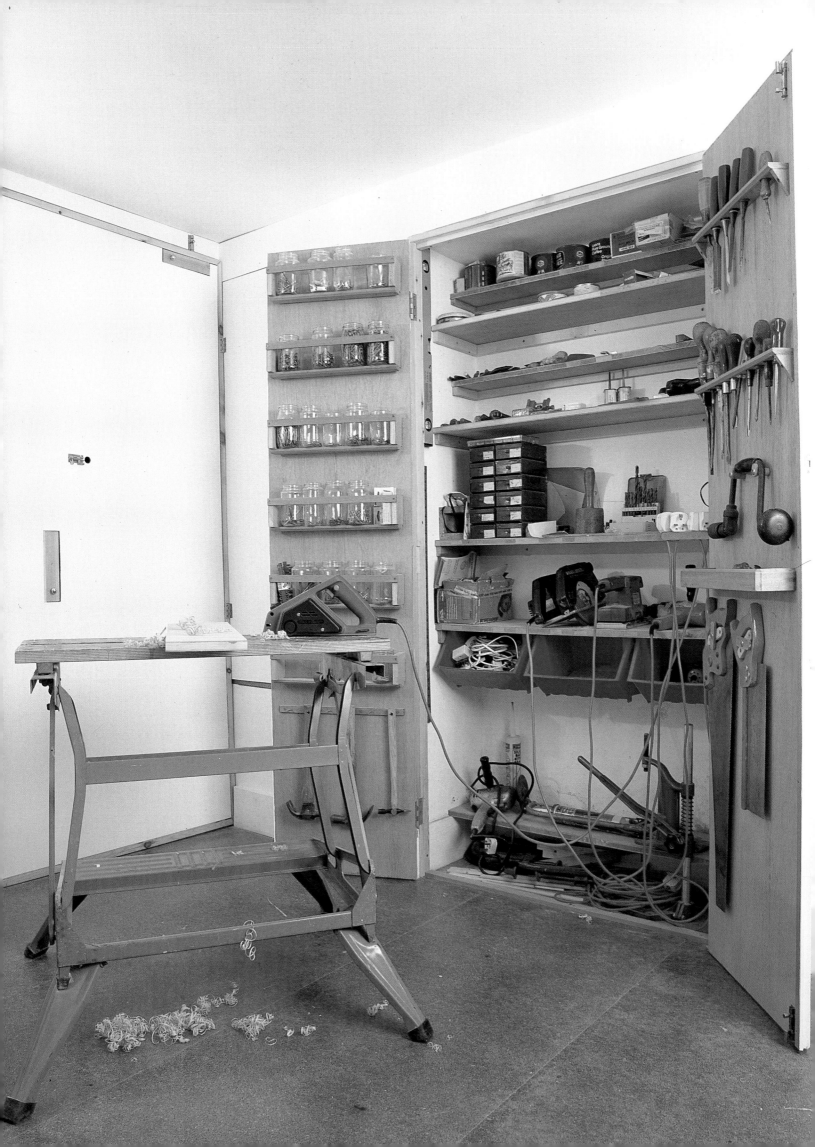

WORKROOMS & HOME OFFICES

LEFT The spare room on page 129 opens out miraculously into this complete carpentry workshop. *The cupboard has been carefully designed so that everything has a place and can be found immediately, with no space wasted. Because there are so many dangerous tools, the doors are locked with childproof locks. Tools should be kept like this in every home with small children.*

More and more people are working from home nowadays, especially (though not exclusively) mothers with young children. But whether you are working to earn money, or just need somewhere to do mending, household maintenance or pursue a particular hobby, you need space to store the tools and a comfortable, well-lit place to use them.

If you feel you need to set aside space for working, think first about whether your home is large enough to give up a whole room or whether you could simply design a work station in an existing room. If you are running a business from your home, tax laws, especially in America, require the space to be clearly separate and used only for business purposes in order for it to be deductible as a business expense.

Before you start, work out how much space you need and whether the children are welcome to come and join you there for quiet pursuits like drawing or doing homework. Assess whether your own requirements would allow them to come and join you for messy pursuits such as painting or collage: if so, you will need washable walls and flooring. On the other hand it may be that you need to keep the place clean and neat, especially if you use it for meetings with clients.

The position of your workroom within the house depends on the type of work and the age of your children. If your children are very small and are being looked after by another adult in your home while you are working, it helps if you don't have to get into the cupboard in order to hear the person on the other end while you are making a business call to Norway.

ABOVE A large home office, created from an upstairs bedroom, has space for five people to work together without getting in each other's way, although it has usually only one occupant. It is often used for homework, sewing, and lots of other activities. The ironing board is left up for all but the most important meetings. With the tables arranged in a U-shape, the person seated in front of the computer is within easy reach of all three surfaces. The blue table is lower for a younger child to use and space has been set aside for the children to store their belongings so they don't become muddled with work in progress.

To avoid this, your workroom should not be positioned too close to rooms mainly used by the rest of the family. A loft or attic conversion is a very economical use of space for someone running a business from home – it doesn't take space away from the family and you are marginally less likely to nip into the office at the weekend just to write one more letter if it means traipsing to the top of the house.

However, if you are looking after the children at the same time as designing a multi-storey car park, it's much easier if they aren't too far away, especially when they are a bit older and only need to know who's eaten all the bread. You may find that a two-way intercom is useful if you need to work when the rest of the family is at home and you don't want to conduct all communications at the tops of your voices.

The amount of space you need depends on what you are doing. You may only need a work station on the landing (see p.24) or a desk in your bedroom (see p.106). With carefully designed storage this can be a very good use of space as a bedroom is scarcely used for most of the day and office equipment and accessories are now well-designed in lots of bright colours, so that your work station needn't look like a still from a 'forties B-movie.

LIGHTING A workroom needs to be filled with light, with special areas lit with task lights for detailed work. A simple angled architect's light is inexpensive and may be adequate on its own, but a track with adjustable spots provides the most flexible system.

WORK SPACE AND STORAGE Somehow you always need more than you have, so allow yourself as much space as you can to work in. No doubt your children will help you fill it, with little presents and paintings and special rocks that are very important and just can't be thrown away. In order to have enough uncluttered working space you need to have good storage and be disciplined about using it. Think hard about what you need to keep, and the best way to organize it, so that there aren't acres of space wasted in cupboards or on shelves. This may be a good place to keep useful bits and pieces that your children could use at some time for collages or fancy dress costumes, for instance.

Use hanging files for any papers that need to be found quickly; piles on the desk that need searching through take up space on your work table and you may find your painstakingly typed Report has been adorned with pictures of Transformers while you were out of the room.

If you have children under five in your home or frequent young visitors of that age, make sure that any sharp cutting tools, abrasives or liquid chemicals are out of reach and locked away.

WORD PROCESSORS AND HOME COMPUTERS Many people now have these at home, for business or simply to manage the household accounts, but with children around you need to be vigilant. Food and drink spilled into the keyboard or printer render most machines unusable – sometimes irreparably. Never leave your computer on when a small child is around without saving your work in progress or you may find three hours' painstaking work wiped out by a second's innocent fiddling.

The cutting table of a dress designer working from home provides everybody with the chance to spread out or embark on enormous school projects. Ceramic floor tiles can be wiped clean after the paint, glue or milk shake has been dropped on the floor (and the principles of gravity discussed) and then been walked in, while the long fluorescent tubes make sure the whole of the table top is lit.

If you've ever worked at home and looked after your children at the same time, you will appreciate how well designed this room is. The steps up to the work space can be used for jumping off as well as for storage. Two of the cupboards hold toys and the other childproofed one contains adult drawing equipment. When the children are playing in the lower part of this room the sculptured head, the fern and the pot of flowers are removed to a place of safety on the upper level.

Don't use fluorescent lights if you regularly work at a VDU as the combination is extremely tiring. Computers can make a small room very hot and stuffy and the more sophisticated don't enjoy a dusty atmosphere, so consider installing air conditioning in your office if you don't have it already, and keep the place spotlessly clean. With children around, this probably means locking the room when not in use.

Finally, computer games are fun but you bought the machine for work, not as a toy for kids. If you're tolerant enough to allow them to use it, set aside a time and stick to it.

ATTICS, CELLARS & GARAGES

ABOVE An attic can be converted into a wonderful child's bedroom once she is old enough not to wake up regularly in the night. This area under the roof housed a large water tank; these have been replaced by four small ones tucked away behind doors under the eaves where it is too low to stand.

Attics, cellars and garages are often used for storing dangerous chemicals and equipment, but they do have marvellous potential as play spaces for older children – probably over eight is a reasonable rule-of-thumb. Suitably adapted, they could for instance be used for a hobby, safe from the destructive fingers of younger members of the family, or just as a more interesting place to take friends.

If you want to give over part of your attic or cellar in this way, it must be made safe. Look around and see if there are any hazards such as low windows, unsafe stairs, exposed insulation, missing floorboards, places to get trapped in or, especially, makeshift wiring or open water tanks. Garages need especially careful thought before you allow them to be used by children (see below).

Remove all potentially dangerous items that you store there. If that's impossible, and your children are of a suitable age and trustworthiness, keep any such equipment well out of reach and explain the potential dangers as graphically as possible. Keep hazardous substances like lawn fertilizer or anti-freeze in a locked cupboard. If you can't do that or aren't prepared to, then it's best to abandon the idea of allowing your children unsupervised access to these areas. If you can make it safe for the over-eights, make sure that younger siblings and visitors are not allowed to wander into the room alone and disrupt everything or hurt themselves.

RIGHT Many houses have attic rooms like this as part of the original interior. The shelves use every inch of space on that wall and act as part of the room decoration. The cork tile floor provides extra insulation and is left as clear as possible for spreading out games.

ATTICS

The space under the roof rafters can be a wonderful area that is often unused except to store those things that you don't really need but can't bear to throw away. An attic that is big enough can be turned into an excellent room, often with a very large floor area, but the sloping ceiling may make the space uncomfortable to use on a daily basis, especially for anyone over 5ft 5in (1.6m). Skylight windows fitted into the slope of the roof are relatively simple to instal to let in light, although you may require local authority planning or zoning permission to do this. Make sure that you have a safety latch fitted because they open from the bottom, and the distance from floor to window may not be very high.

A full-blown attic conversion into an extra room is a major undertaking, although there are building firms who specialize in this. You may need planning or zoning permission, and careful consideration has to be given, among other things, to the position of the extra flight of stairs required, to strengthening the floor, fire regulations and insulation.

If you don't need to or can't afford a complete conversion but just want to allow your children to use part of the space as a den, there are still certain things that may need to be done. If there aren't any floorboards but just insulation in between the joists you will need to put in some sort of flooring. This will require stengthening the ceiling joists for the room below. They aren't as strong as floor joists, even if your children weigh only 75lb (34kg) each, and when there are several of them jumping up and down, the weight is enormous.

If the use is only to be occasional and for children, it is not necessary to have proper floorboards fitted – strong sheets of blockboard or plywood would do just as well, which could be stained or painted in a vivid colour. What is important is to enclose completely any fibreglass insulation because, although it looks rather invitingly cosy, it is very irritating to the skin and it is dangerous to inhale the fibres.

The stairs going up to the attic must have a secure hand rail as they are often quite steep. If you use a ladder it should be one specially made for the purpose. A retractable ladder is neat – you can now obtain ladders with spring mechanisms which even a child can let down safely.

An attic is usually very dusty; as much of this comes from the roof itself you could line the rafters simply with insulating board or even pin up swathes of flame-retardant cloth to make an exciting tent-like environment. Even so, the space will need regular cleaning if the dirt is not to be trailed through your home every time the children come down, so make sure access for cleaning equipment isn't too difficult.

Even if you have a window put in the roof, some alternative light source will be necessary, and an intercom is also useful since heat insulation is also an extremely efficient sound insulator. It is helpful to have a couple of double sockets fitted and a lighting circuit, with special attention to safety. Have any existing electrical systems checked before you allow children to use an attic regularly. White fairy lights hung from the rafters are magical, but an adjustable work light or spots would be needed if the room is used for homework or a hobby.

Roof spaces can be pretty cold – if your roof insulation is between the joists it will stop warm air rising up into the roof cavity. If you have a full conversion the insulation is put behind the wall lining; if the room is only to be used as a den then your heat source could either be another radiator from the central heating system or a properly installed electric heater without an exposed element.

However tempting it may be to them, explain to your children why they must never take candles or matches up into the attic. When they are young, these should anyway be kept out of their reach at all times but as your children get older childproofing relaxes and things that are dangerous become more available. It is sometimes difficult always to keep everything locked away, and there has to come a time when children learn to be responsible for themselves, but of course you still need to be vigilant.

If the children have their own electrical equipment in the attic, such as an electric keyboard or cassette player, plus any lighting, you will need to check each night that everything has been turned off, and have a large notice pinned somewhere near the exit that reminds them to do this off when they leave.

CELLARS

A really good creepy cellar that is dripping wet or four feet from floor to ceiling – as opposed to a full basement (see p. 71) – can be a brilliant place to play, so long as you have checked that it is safe and there is no danger of getting locked in. As with attics, fairy lights can be very atmospheric in a cellar, but you should instal the ones that are specially designed for outside use, in case any damp gets in. A wine cellar may need a good lock on it when your children are older to make sure not too much of the vintage port gets 'borrowed'. This may seem uncharitable but some teenagers who are used to the idea that what's yours is theirs, don't know where to stop.

GARAGES

A garage which is in constant use is not recommended as a place for children to play, especially if you also use it for car maintenance or as a workshop. However occasionally it might be worth moving the car out and letting older children have the run of it for band rehearsals or remote control car races. If you do allow this sort of usage, then dangerous items must be stored off the floor.

GARDENS & BACKYARDS

A garden or backyard designed with children in mind can be used all the year round so that it becomes the equivalent of an extra room, where it is safe for your children to play and generally let off steam. A well thought out garden is a restful place for a parent because you will not need to stop the children constantly from standing on the plants or eating the poisonous berries. In addition, it is not necessary to cover it with play equipment for it to be a place for children to enjoy.

The size of your garden, the age of your children, and how much time you have to spend gardening, will all dictate the way you use it. You would probably like your garden to look good but may not have the encyclopaedic knowledge or time that is needed to plan and maintain it. Acres of flower beds need planting, weeding and watering, and they take up valuable playing space. With children in the family, it is better to plant small areas with shrubs and perennials that look after themselves and a few annuals to add extra colour, then leave the rest as lawn and terrace to play on.

If your children are under four at the time you are planning your garden, keep it on one level if possible (or have a level area if you live on the side of a hill) so that they can have the freedom to run about safely without falling down steps or off low walls onto paving stones. Keep it simple until their bikes are too big to ride in the garden.

A simple sign on this welcoming gate saying 'please shut the gate' will go some way to jogging people's memory as they come and go, but there should be no easy access to the front garden for a small child. The seats on either side of the gate for weary passers-by are a kind thought.

Many children enjoy having their own growing area. It could be decorated with carefully placed shells or large pebbles, too big for a young child to swallow, interspersed with plants that germinate quickly, flower profusely throughout the season, aren't poisonous and are hardy enough to survive neglect and over-watering. (See p. 157).

FRONT GARDENS

Front gardens should be out of bounds to young children if they are anywhere near a road. If there is any possibility of a child straying into the front garden there should always be a fence or some other barrier to ensure that she cannot wander into the road. The latch on the gate must be childproof or at very least out of reach, on the outside of the gate. A self-shutting gate on a spring is only worth investing in if small fingers can't be trapped in it. A 'Please shut the gate' sign will alert people to shut it more often. Make your front garden safe before your child is crawling, so that you don't get caught out one day and find her in the road talking to the postman.

SMALL GARDENS

If your garden is to be used by your children as a playspace and there isn't very much room in it, you must resign yourself to the fact that you need to leave as much area for them to play

It is impossible to grow grass in a shady garden this size, so bricks have been laid on their sides in a herringbone design. This warm, attractive all-weather surface offsets the plants and provides excellent biking facilities for a small child. There is even a tree to ride around.

in as possible while they are young and keep the flower beds to defined spaces where they can't be trodden on. Raised beds are one answer, so long as they are positioned next to grass rather than paving stones.

It is difficult, however, to grow grass in a very small area especially if your children are constantly playing on it. Although it is pleasant to have grass to sit on, you just have to admit defeat if your children want to play football or ride bikes, because all there will be is a mud patch, no matter what kind of grass you have. In these circumstances it is better to give up the unequal struggle and have your whole back yard paved. You can channel the children's energy through a basketball hoop attached to an outside wall of the house or garage, not too near the windows. Another game for older children which doesn't take up too much space but develops sports skills is swing or tetherball, and a badminton net suspended over a paved area could double for volley ball.

In a very small garden concentrate on space-saving container grown plants and flowering climbers which provide colour on a vertical rather than a horizontal plane. Avoid prickly shrubs such as roses, berberis or cotoneaster as a child will inevitably choose one of them to trip against when running about in the limited space available. If you are particularly keen on roses, there are some which are practically thornless so it is worth asking your local garden centre or nurseryman for advice.

BALCONIES AND ROOF GARDENS

Although a balcony or roof garden may be the only private outdoor space available to city dwellers, a small child should never be allowed onto one alone. A stair-gate may be useful if you like to have the door open that leads on to these potentially dangerous areas. The door opening on to a balcony or roof garden should be self-closing and have a lock that is too high to reach even if a child stands on a chair. Alternatively make sure it is locked with a key that hangs near

Many town house gardens are long and thin which might restrict their flexibility for children. A way round this is to divide the garden into distinct areas – three equal parts in this case – each with a different purpose. Originally the garden was flat and laid to lawn, while the children were small, but as they grew the garden was re-landscaped to provide all-weather play. The end of the garden with the swing is given over mostly for their use. The central area has stepping stones across the grass, where it has the heaviest use, otherwise it would end up with bald patches, and the area nearest the house is used for eating, sunbathing and entertaining. Paving stones are fun to chalk on, with blackboard chalk, but it does get washed away when it rains.

A bamboo thicket has been grown in a circle and the centre constantly thinned out to leave a small clearing in the middle as a secret camp for panda hunting or whatever. With a bit of forethought and not too much heavy pruning, large shrubs can make wonderful places to play.

A roof terrace often catches the sun when it has gone from ground level and it can be a lovely place to make a garden.

This roof terrace was only installed once the children of the household were old enough to be responsible out there on their own. Access is from an upstairs landing, and the door shuts automatically and is always locked when no one is using it. The fence has been designed so that the horizontal struts are too far away from each other for a young child's legs to straddle even if he were to stand on the plant pots.

the door but out of reach, and maybe even out of sight to dangerously adventurous children. However, if your balcony is an escape route in an emergency the key needs to be accessible to everyone in a position of responsibility, so make sure they know where it is, including older children.

It is very difficult to erect a fence or railing that is impossible to climb, but you need to be as prepared as possible to avoid the unthinkable happening if your child does manage to get out onto the balcony or roof alone. It is also much more relaxing when you want to sit out there yourself if you don't have to worry continuously about pulling him away from the fence.

If the existing fencing or railings are not safe, or the rails are too wide apart, then they should be replaced. Different types of fencing present different problems. If you have a picket fence, the horizontal struts should be at least 20in (50cm) apart so that a child would have to have long legs to climb over, and the vertical slats should be no more than 2⅜in (60mm) apart, the same as a cot, so that small heads cannot get stuck between them. There should be no space at the bottom to wriggle under.

If you are worried about losing the view, toughened clear plastic surrounds at least 3ft (93cm) high provide uninterrupted vision, while diamond shaped trellis securely attached to the balcony rails allows light to filter attractively through. To avoid the trellis being used as a climbing frame, plant a round-bottomed container (that would tip if climbed on) in front with a fast-growing climber like Clematis Montana, or a prickly rambling rose. This should put off all but the most determined, but it needs to be planned before your children can even walk so the plants have a chance to grow big enough to become a deterrent.

If you have a roof garden with a low wall around it, attach lengths of diamond-shaped trellis to upright posts, and secure these firmly to the inside of the wall to support wind-resistant climbing plants. Trellis is not very strong and can still be climbed but the extra height means there is less incentive, unlike a wall which is just the right height to balance on, but just happens to be three storeys up.

LARGER GARDENS

If you are lucky enough to have a large garden you will know that it takes a lot of time to keep it looking good and under control. However, children love hiding places, and you may already have the makings of a secret garden, behind hedges, under a weeping tree or in a large bamboo thicket or shrubbery.

One style of garden design which suits a family is to divide the garden into 'rooms' – the 'walls' of which are planted as different types of hedge or shrubbery, which can be grown to a reasonable height to protect special areas from flying balls. Obviously this requires long-term planning but it is an excellent way of providing clear demarcation lines between the area where football can be played and bikes ridden with impunity and areas where your prize rare plants can have a chance to thrive unmolested. You may also have space to set aside as an environmental area, perhaps among fruit trees like an old-fashioned orchard, which can be allowed to grow wild to show children how nature takes its course.

A large garden allows plenty of scope for play equipment (see below). If you are designating a specific play area, position it within sight of the house so that you can intervene when the children are ganging up on each other, or doing something dangerous. If you have a large lawn, this can be a wonderful resource for games, but the same problems can arise as with small gardens, so decide whether you are looking for acres of unspoilt greensward or don't mind your garden cluttered with sports equipment like Wembley or Shea Stadium.

SURFACES FOR PLAY AREAS

<u>HARD SURFACES</u> A wooden deck or paving stones make a good surface for play. These are usually laid near the house and can still be played on in wet weather. Sand can easily be swept up from around the sand pit and a small bike is easy to ride on this sort of terrace area. If you have grass, it should be complemented with a hard surface so that the grass can be made out of bounds when the weather is wet.

<u>BARK</u> Bark chippings are the ideal ground covering under play equipment (see below). Although not cheap, it is much safer and softer to land on than paving stones or even grass. As it is an expensive material it is best to put a climbing frame on grass and save the bark for under the swing, where grass gets rubbed away to leave a muddy or hard surface to fall on.

Bark needs to be contained otherwise it spreads everywhere and the effect is lost. Centre the swing on an area of chippings, leaving a 2yd (1.8m) extra margin either side of the swing, and 9yds (7m) from front and back to allow for the arc of the swing. The extra width around the swing is needed because children tend to play near it.

There are two ways of using the bark. One is to dig a hole 12ins (300mm) deep, and build a treated timber edging round it, 14ins (350mm) high. Line the bottom of the hole with a breathable textile layer, which can be bought from a builders' merchant. It stops the bark picking up the moisture from the ground and disintegrating. The material should be good quality, play-grade bark and be 12ins (300mm) deep. Paint the raised outside edge of the timber with white paint to stop children from tripping over it.

Alternatively, if the swing is set into paving stones, you can build the bark tray on the top, which is much easier. The 14ins (350mm) retaining edge of treated timber should be secured into the paving stones at about 1yd (900mm) intervals. If you choose to build it this way there will need to be one step up somewhere along the edge. The bark area will need to be raked periodically. Bark is also used for keeping weeds down and retaining moisture in flowerbeds, but this quality is not strong enough to play on.

Public play areas often use bark, and the more expensive alternative of rubberized all-weather matting, which usually comes in 2ft (60cm) squares, and is designed to soften the impact of a falling child. This is undoubtedly the best surface for landing on, but unfortunately it is prohibitively expensive for ordinary domestic use. (See Addresses p.172.)

<u>LAWNS</u> A grassed area for children's use needs to be hard-wearing, so look for seed or turf suitable for a utility lawn. These usually contain a mixture of meadow grasses, fescue and rye, and should not be too closely mown. If you are laying a new lawn explain to your local supplier or contractor that you want a hard-wearing lawn for children's use.

If your children are under ten it is better not to try to seed a lawn, unless there is a lot of other space for them to play in, because it just takes too long to grow before it is strong enough for use – eight to ten weeks depending on conditions. This is a bore since the best time for sowing is April, so the lawn would be out of bounds for most of the spring and summer.

Laying turf is a less frustrating though more expensive option with children around as they should be laid between September and February to allow them time to settle before the growing season. A new lawn needs watering once or twice a week with a sprinkler to avoid shrinkage.

Lawns that are walked on a lot may develop bald patches where they are most used. If you can identify these places insert 'stepping stones' and encourage your family to use them. Stepping stones must be the shortest route from A to B otherwise they just won't be used.

Make sure your children do not walk on the lawn when it is very wet or if there has been snow or frost. This is when your hard surface is very useful because they can still play outside on it. It is safer if your children are not nearby when the lawn is being mown as flying debris can come out fast and it is very painful if it hits you. This is particularly true if you use a high-powered trimmer.

<u>ABOVE</u> *One of the simplest but most popular garden games for a hot day is to run a hose along a thick plastic sheet so that the children can slide along it. (These can be bought commercially.) It is also fun to place it at the end of a slide and run the hose from the top of the slide for daredevil speed sliding.*

<u>LEFT</u> *There is no need to go to the park when you have a proper play area like this. It is situated at the side of the house in a large garden, and makes use of bark chippings under the swing, easily the softest surface to land on. The large sand pit has a wide surround so that the children can sit comfortably on the edge and build sand castles without all the sand ending up on the outside. As this sand pit is permanent it has been put near the hedge so that there is some shade to play in when it is very hot.*

ABOVE *Children are fascinated by hammocks and spend hours lying and swinging in them – one advantage is that two children can enjoy the game together. These two fruit trees have been planted at exactly the right distance apart to hang a hammock, slung low enough for children to be able to get into it easily. Behind it is a path that has been thoughtfully laid right round the lawn, perfect for riding a small bike round and round and round.*

PATHS A path through and around a lawn can be a wonderful place to ride a tricycle. The ideal path is made up of paving stones, about two feet wide, designed to make a round trip so that your child doesn't have to stop and turn the bike round. Concrete or tarmac would do as well but are not nearly so aesthetic. If you have a ground level change, connect it by a gentle slope rather than steps, but make sure children will not crash into anything at the bottom.

Gravel or shingle paths or driveways are not very practical with small children around. Children are fascinated by the stones and tend to throw them around or put them in their mouths, and they can hurt themselves if they fall on them. Gravel tends to stick to shoes and comes into the house. It also breaks the lawnmower if any of it gets onto the grass.

TREES Check that any tree in your garden that is even remotely possible to climb is safe. Remove any dead branches regularly. The hardest thing about climbing a tall tree is

RIGHT *A garden laid on the slope of a hill provides a wonderful site for a tree house that is built around the tree rather than in it. There is more space to play in and it is easier and safer than constructing it in the tree itself. There is a platform and a shelter where you can spot your enemies from miles away; the dovecot shown on page 145 is about 50 feet (12m) away and makes another good camp from which to do battle.*

A pond in a garden is lovely, it is soothing and can be fascinating as it is a haven for garden wildlife such as frogs and toads, birds, dragonflies and fish. However it does need to be made safe by covering it with stiff wire mesh. This not only stops children falling in but prevents balls and other missiles being aimed at your prize water lilies.

getting down again. If you have older, agile children, one way round this is to fix a fireman's pole or rope from as high up in the tree as possible. (If it is a pole, make sure it is firmly anchored in the ground.) The pole or rope should be fixed to the branch above the one your children stand on so that they can grab it easily rather than having to lower themselves on to it. Make sure your children and their friends know how to come down hand-over-hand or they will burn their hands.

A tree house is many children's dream. If you have a tree sturdy enough and the right shape to accommodate one, you must ensure that the house itself is secure in the tree and that the way up and down from it is safe and easy to use. An acceptable alternative to a tree house is to build one on to a high wooden platform which can double as a climbing frame.

FOUNTAINS AND FISHPONDS A fountain with a basin surround or a pond are not a good idea with very small children; it is better to wait until they are older. If you inherit a pond and don't want to take it out, you must cover it with rigid, close-mesh netting. Having said that, a pond is a wonderful resource for children (see p.158) since it attracts birds and can accommodate fish, tadpoles, frogs and toads, and some beautiful aquatic plants. If well designed, a small fountain with water that plays onto a pedestal and simply runs away into a conduit to be recycled round again is endlessly fascinating and need not be a hazard.

STORAGE

Toys that are kept in the garden are often quite large and while they do become dirty and worn after a while, they can last for years. To avoid having to live with rusting toys hanging around the garden, store them out of sight and under cover, preferably somewhere separate from where your gardening equipment is kept. A low lean-to shed no more than 2ft 6in (75cm) deep, with an easy-to-open door is ideal, with light toys like plastic wheelbarrows or lawnmowers hanging on the wall, and heavier items like bikes, trolleys and trucks on the ground.

However, this may not be possible and unfortunately your children's toys may have to share space in the garden shed. As so many garden tools and products are dangerous or poisonous, keep all the sharp instruments and chemicals out of sight and well out of reach. Keep the toys near the door so that your child doesn't need to go right into the shed or garage. As many toys as possible should be stored under the work bench or hung on the wall near the ground. There should always be a clear passage to the back of the shed; there is nothing more irritating than scraping your shins on the old trike on the way to retrieve last year's narcissus bulbs. Throw or give away out-grown toys before you find your children haven't used them for the past two years, while you have been suffering their presence needlessly.

Long-handled tools, such as rakes or hoes, are best hung horizontally on a wall on large hooks. Position them carefully so that they are out of reach of a child but an adult can get them down comfortably and safely. Electrical equipment should not be used with small children around in case you get distracted and forget to turn the power off when you are dealing with the distraction.

GARDEN EQUIPMENT

<u>TABLES AND CHAIRS</u> Eating in the garden is such a pleasure on a beautiful day. Any furniture needs to be weather-proof and should not pinch small fingers when it is being collapsed. Reclining chairs and swing seats are always in demand, so if you want a chance to sit in one, without a fight, have enough to go round.

<u>WATER</u> An outside tap is essential to a successful garden. If watering is difficult you don't do it as much as you need to and the plants show it. Small children in particular enjoy watering, although not all the water ends up on the flowers. A hose with a sprinkler is wonderful fun to play under: running in and out of the spray produces lots of screams and giggles, although all too often it means wet clothes as well.

Eating outside can be quite an adventure in this garden. Deep in the undergrowth you'd hardly know the table was there except for the umbrella, which provides plenty of shade for hot summer lunches. There are enough chairs for an instant party at this round table.

A pretty, chalet-style summer house, which was bought from a garden centre, has been set up mainly for the children's use at the bottom of a lovely town garden. It is positioned in the shade except in the early morning to avoid it becoming too hot inside. It acts as an extra playroom, and on warm nights the children sleep in it and have their breakfast at the table outside. There is a swing hanging from the pergola next to it, which in a year or two will be completely covered by a grape vine.

BARBECUES Almost everything tastes delicious cooked on a barbecue, but with children around you do have to be vigilant, there must be someone watching it all the time and it should not be set up in a thoroughfare or too near to the house. If you normally keep a garden spray filled with water handy for dousing the flames of an over-enthusiastic charcoal barbecue, keep a special one marked 'BARBECUE ONLY' in indelible ink to make sure you don't flavour the food with aphid spray or something equally unsavoury by mistake.

Propane gas barbecues are becoming increasingly popular since they require no preparation and are ready to use within a few minutes of lighting. There is no ash residue to get rid of either. However, most models are self-starting, like a stove, so should not be left standing around unattended since a child could easily turn one on.

LIGHTING Lights in a garden add an extra dimension and extend the time it can be used. If installed with thought, they can enhance your garden enormously.

Fairy lights strung in a tree need not only be kept for parties, they can be a permanent fixture, but must be specially made to be used outside. Exterior lamp fittings can be attached to the wall, to trees or be planted in the flowerbeds. The best lighting for a family garden is high up, attached to the house or a wall. Outdoor lighting is usually rather powerful so you have to make sure you position the fixtures where they are not going to blind somebody standing in the garden when they are on.

The more light fittings you have the more of your garden will be used after dark. When your children are older, it might be worth investing in a portable fitting fixed on a spike, that can be moved around to light a forgotten area or an illicit game of Trivial Pursuit at the bottom of the garden.

PLAY EQUIPMENT

Garden play equipment increases the potential of your garden as a play area for children. It doesn't have to be very complicated or expensive – it's amazing how much mileage children can get out of a very simple swing – but it does need to be safe. Check that the equipment is in good repair from time to time. Listed below are just some of the items that can be bought, or made. But before you invest in some fairly expensive equipment or give in to pleas from your children, find out what older children have enjoyed and what was a nine-day wonder.

SAND PIT   A sand pit provides hours of fun for small children and it is surprising for how many years older children continue to find pleasure in sand. A sand pit is of special benefit in a small garden which is limited in what it can offer to a child. The sand pit could be portable, so that it can be put away for the winter, or made a permanent fixture. Either way, it should be big enough for two children to sit in and a well-fitting lid is essential otherwise all the neighbourhood cats will think it is there just for their use!

This cleverly designed sandpit combines a detachable, folding cover with a low garden bench. The central section of the cover can be removed to leave a seat on both sides of the sandpit to sit on when the children are playing in it.

A sand pit needs careful positioning on or within a hard surface. If it is too near to the door there will be a constant trail of sand into the house, so the best place is within sight of the house but not too close, in a partially-shaded position.

Only use pre-cleaned silver sand, available from garden centres; building sand contains additives which stain your children and their clothes yellow and can irritate skin. Top up the sand regularly and sprinkle it with water during very dry weather. It will need changing a couple of times each summer or you will find that you are living with a sand pit that is never used, or your children will be making mud pies rather than sand castles as garden soil inevitably becomes mixed in.

Perfecting your skills at basket ball at home can give you the edge over the people you are trying to impress – and might just get you into the team.

SWINGS A swing can be popular for a number of years so it is a good investment in a family garden. Position it so that the swing doesn't cross a path when in use and is at a reasonable distance from a sand pit or other play equipment – small children can't see the danger of a swing in use and tend just to run past it.

Free-standing swings should be anchored firmly, preferably on a surface of bark (see above). If you hang a swing from a tree make sure that the supporting branch is strong and healthy, and that the ropes cannot move along the branch when the swing is in use. It should be positioned well away from the trunk so there is no danger of collision during use.

The swing seat should be made of plastic; if a child falls off and is hit by the seat or walks into it, plastic does not do as much damage as a wooden seat.

CLIMBING FRAME OR JUNGLE GYM A climbing frame is a sizeable investment so should be designed to last for several years. The bars should be near enough together for the child to climb it when she is small and another part of the frame should be challenging for older children. One solution might be to choose a manufactured system that can have extra parts bolted on later. One plastic system is capable of being dismantled and reassembled in any number of shapes; it does not rust and is not cold to the hands. It is good for small gardens as quite compact shapes can be constructed, and it can be dismantled and stored in a garage or shed.

Climbing frames can be set into grass, bark or sand. Avoid concrete or paving stones, as they are very hard to fall on.

TRAMPOLINES Full-size trampolines should only be used under trained supervision, but a keep-fit 'Jogger' or small portable trampoline is a good alternative. The appeal for children often wears off fairly quickly, but it's good exercise for the rest of the family, and even granny could benefit!

SPORTS EQUIPMENT Items like goal posts, basketball hoops, badminton nets and the like are a must for the avid player, they do improve skills. Position the goal posts where the least amount of damage can be done by the ball when a goal hasn't been scored.

SLIDES Initially, a lot of fun can be had from a slide, but the novelty can wear off quite quickly. Make sure that whatever the children land on is soft and firm – rubber tiles are the best surface if you can afford them, but even pieces of old carpet would do. Buy the size of slide that you feel is appropriate for

the age of your children, but with an eye to the future. Slides can often be bought to be compatible with a climbing frame, and this increases their interest.

PADDLING POOLS In hot weather a paddling pool can be enjoyed by all the children and the odd adult too. The best type is the one which fits onto a rigid frame – inflatable paddling pools rarely last more than one season without puncturing. Most pools are collapsible, but make sure that they are dry before you fold them away otherwise they smell. Remember that a child can drown in four inches of water, so they need constant supervision. Always empty the pool when the children have finished using it, to make sure no one goes back into it when you are not watching.

SWIMMING POOLS They are both a blessing and a bugbear with small children; the children love being in them, but can't be left alone at all in case of an accident. Define the rules right from the start and apply them to all children, regardless of age or swimming ability.

    If you are thinking of installing a swimming pool and your children are very small look for one with easy steps and a shallow end that is 2ft (60cm) deep so that they can stand.

The slide set into the hill next to the steps is a very good way to use a slope. With an instant swing attached to a fallen tree, every opportunity has been taken to use the natural resources of this garden for the children's benefit.

This beautiful veranda with its white wicker furniture and blue painted floor has a fresh cool feeling, a sanctuary out of the midday sun. A swinging seat is every child's dream so although it might incite arguments it will give great pleasure too. The veranda is handy for the swimming pool, which is surrounded by a picturesque but childproof white picket fence.

This gives an immense feeling of confidence to a child who is learning to swim, speeding up the whole process enormously.

The pool surround must have a non-slip surface and the children should be told never to run or play about near the edge of the pool. Tricycles or other toys on wheels should never be ridden near the pool either, as it is incredibly easy to ride straight in. Read them the riot act if there is any pushing in.

The pool must be fully enclosed, high enough not to be climbed over. The barrier can be made more attractive by growing climbing plants over it. A longer term idea is to plant a wide hedge in front of a fence, which could be removed when the hedge is fully grown. All the doors and gates leading to the pool should have a self-closing and latching system out of the reach of children under eight. This also protects the family pets, especially dogs – if they fall in, they often can't find the steps to get out and will swim round and round until exhausted.

No one should ever swim alone. Even adults should swim with a 'spotter' nearby: if they always do this then children are more likely to follow their example. If possible, the adults who are supervising the pool should be trained in artificial respiration and have done a life-saving course. At the very least they should be able to swim competently. Keep a first aid book near the pool that includes resuscitation techniques. All this may seem over-cautious but it is important to be prepared.

Keep a life-saving pole on each side of the pool and make sure they are not moved or played with. Arm-bands are not life-savers but they would keep a small child that falls in afloat, so it is wise to insist that small children and non-swimmers always wear them in the vicinity of the pool.

Diving boards or slides should not be installed unless your pool is deep enough, that is, at least 6ft (1.8m) at the deep end. Ideally a slide should run into even deeper water, as sliding down head first means going quite deep and a child could hit her head on the bottom. No above ground pool is deep enough for a slide. Never let a child dive in at the shallow end.

A pool cover keeps the warmth of the water in and the debris out. Make it clear to your own and all visiting children that they must never stand on the cover. Most flexible 'bubble' covers can be simply removed on a roller with the handle – it should be rolled back completely when you are using the pool to ensure no one gets trapped under it.

Use only unbreakable plates and cups near the pool and try to keep any food as far away as possible from the pool edge – it's no fun swimming in bits of half-eaten hot dog. Alcohol, drugs (prescribed or otherwise) and swimming pools don't mix; older experimenting teenagers must be made aware of the dangers and reminded of the false courage alcohol gives you. Even the pool side can be dangerous to the inexperienced drinker. Adults who have 'had one or two' have slower reflexes and in just the same way as it is dangerous to drink and drive, it is dangerous to drink and swim especially if you are tired. Have a swim, then have a drink.

Any electrical appliances that you need to use near the pool, such as hedge clippers or lawn mowers, should be fitted with a circuit breaker. Even a telephone can cause electrocution in a swimming pool, and all pool chemicals should be kept locked away, out of the reach of all children.

CHILDREN'S GARDENS

There is no particular age that children need to be before they can have their own garden. At any age they can be enthusiastic for five minutes and then lose interest in the whole idea. If their interest is real they will be badgering you to help or to have their own patch so it is worth nurturing even if the enthusiasm wanes after a while, because they will have learned something from it.

Choose a sunny sheltered spot no bigger than 5ft by 3ft (1.5m by 1m) so that they can reach into the centre of it. Anything bigger will overwhelm the child from the start and he will give up trying. Try to position the plot near to the outside tap and hose, as water is heavy to carry.

If you are starting from scratch the plot needs to be dug over in the autumn. This is hard work so it is probably best to work with your child on this so that you are on hand when energy and resolve drain away. In the spring add rotted manure or compost to make the area more fertile.

Because children's boredom level is rather high, it is important to choose plants which are relatively easy and quick to grow and reward the child with a showy display of brightly coloured blooms throughout the summer. This is the true sign of success and will also be marvellous to look at. Remind your child to water the garden daily in a dry spell; the best time is the late afternoon once the sun has gone off the patch. Help your child to feed the plants once a week with a good liquid fertilizer – tomato food is good – and explain that removing the dead flowers helps to lengthen the flowering time.

If the bed is in front of a wall or fence, plant the tallest plants at the back, medium in the middle and small and trailing plants in the front. If the bed is an island shape, group the plants in a pyramid, with the tallest in the middle. Many of the plants listed below are annuals, but it is probably best in the first year to buy plants rather than growing from seed, to avoid disappointment. Many of these can just as easily be grown in containers or window-boxes.

Decorated stones, especially large round flat ones that you could collect on a trip to the beach, are fun to paint with water resistant paint or felt tip pens, and along with shells help to enliven the garden especially in winter.

Children who are interested in gardening enjoy eating the fruits of their labours, but you will have spent a lot of time telling them not to eat plants and berries in the garden so it is wise not to let small children grow edible plants in their own gardens at first. Save that pleasure until they are older and more discriminating. Strawberries, radishes, parsley, black-berries, watermelons and courgettes (zucchini) are all relative-ly easy to grow, as are tomatoes, though remember that the leaves and stems are poisonous. Bush tomatoes are particularly rewarding as they grow more or less anywhere and don't need as much attention as more conventional varieties.

TREES

Some trees can be grown successfully from seed. Acorns, hazelnuts, beechnuts, sycamore seeds and horse chestnuts all take well, but shouldn't be eaten. Fruit pips from apples and oranges can be grown but the plants will not bear fruit, which may be frustrating for a child.

EASY PLANTS FOR A CHILD TO GROW	
TALL AND CLIMBING	
Tulips	Sunflower
Daffodils	Sweet Pea
Cosmos	Cornflower
Geranium	Petunia
MEDIUM	
Scyalla	Marigold
Begonia	Nemesia
Buzy Lizzie	Snapdragon
Candytuft	Stocks
Clarkia	Zinnia
LOW	
Snowdrops	Nasturtium
Crocus	Senecio
Alyssum	Pansy
Lobelia	

Plant the seed in a 6in (15cm) diameter pot in a sandy compost or light loam by pushing it about 1in (25mm) down from the surface of the soil. Then cover it and put the pot outside to germinate. Don't water it during the winter. When the seedling is about 1in (25mm) tall find a place in the garden to plant it. Be very careful that there is enough room around for it to grow to its full height. Your own garden may well be too small and once it gets going you don't get another chance as the roots descend as far down as the branches grow up in some species!

Planting a tree seed is a nice idea when a baby is born – the tree will grow to maturity with the child. However, saplings need some protection so consult a gardening book or tree specialist as the tree grows.

ENCOURAGING WILDLIFE

A garden needn't just be a playspace for your children, it can also provide them with opportunities to look at various kinds of wildlife at close quarters. You can encourage a variety of wildlife into even the smallest city garden if you plant the trees, shrubs and flowers which attract them. If you have room, patches of uncultivated ground and unpruned thickets provide undisturbed cover for breeding birds and small animals, and even a balcony can boast a bird table or feeder and container-grown flowers to entice butterflies and bees.

At some time of their childhood, most young people develop a fascination with creepy crawly creatures such as insects, spiders and worms. Try to curb your own distaste if necessary, and provide them with a magnifying glass instead for close inspection. It may result in a life-long interest.

However, creating a nature reserve in your garden is more complicated than not mowing the lawn or leaving the patch of nettles for the butterflies (see below). There is a lot to discover so it is best to find out from your children's school or read a book devoted to the subject (see the Bibliography on page 172). Of course, if you use chemical pesticides and fertilizers in your garden you will have no wildlife.

BIRDS

Birds need little encouragement to come into your garden. Simply provide them with food (on a cat-proof bird table), a bird bath and perhaps a nesting box. Birds of course love berry-bearing trees and shrubs – hawthorn, blackberry and rowan are among those with berries that aren't poisonous to humans.

A bird table can be made or bought very easily. It can be hung from a tree or screwed into the top of a post, high enough for any cats not to be able to pick the birds off while they are preoccupied with feeding.

Position the table or feeder where it can easily be seen from the house but far enough from any neighbouring wall from which a cat could pounce. All garden birds will be delighted to find sunflower seeds in the bird feeder and large sacks can be bought inexpensively at pet stores, garden centres and the like. Try to avoid the seed mixtures sold in food markets, they contain few sunflower seeds and are not particularly cheap. In the winter, the birds will appreciate suet scraps hung in a mesh bag; another enjoyable way to feed birds is to hang pine

This bird table is designed just as much to be looked at as a place to feed the birds, and its charm adds to an already beautiful garden.

Before the doves had a chance to settle into their new home the children had found the little entrance at the back and claimed squatters' rights, so the doves will not be asked to move in until the present occupiers have got fed up with the game.

BIRD TABLE

A bird table that hangs from a branch is not only easier to make but is harder for predators to penetrate. Position it so that it can be seen from the house. This bird table can also be put up on a balcony by suspending it from a bracket for hanging baskets.

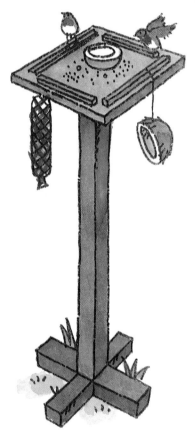

A bird table on a pedestal can be put nearer the house, but it does take up more room and can be knocked over if it is in a thoroughfare. Keep it away from any high vantage points like walls.

cones spread with peanut butter. Birds come to rely on being fed at a particular place and time, so be consistent if possible and they will reward you with their presence. Some may even become quite tame.

A bird bath is important all year round for birds to both drink and wash in. The best shape is low and flat with sloping edges for the birds to hop on to. Change the water regularly, and do not allow it to freeze in the winter – birds can die of thirst when their normal source of drinking water is frozen. A good method is to float a small ball in the water; this works very well except in very severe frosts, but you should check every day in any case. Birds may also have a sandbath in the sand pit if the sand is completely dry, but they will fly away if they sense they are being observed. If it does happen it is delightful to watch, if your children can stay still long enough.

A nest box can make observing a family of birds both possible and fascinating. You can build one yourself, or buy one at a garden centre, preferably recommended by a bird society. Never use anything but wood to make a nest box. Fix the box on a tree trunk in a sheltered place away from prevailing winds and out of direct sunshine, but where you can see it. It can be attached to a tree as low as the height of a small child standing on a set of kitchen steps. This way you know that it will be possible for children to look inside at the nest.

The main problem in built-up areas will be the neighbourhood cats who will pick off any fledglings that fall to the ground. It is quite difficult to encourage birds at all if you have a predatory cat who will reasonably believe that anything flying around its territory will be fair game. However, they can coexist, but you may have to raise the height of the box and forego the excitement of looking directly into it. In more rural, wooded areas squirrels can be a nuisance as they will steal eggs if given a chance, and all fledglings and young birds are at risk from owls and hawks.

If a pair of nesting birds do take up residence, it is best to watch the nest building process from a distance so they aren't frightened away before they have finished. Eggs are usually laid in the morning so count the eggs in the afternoon.

Always wait until the parents have vacated the box before looking into it. If you are not sure if they are there, shake the tree very slightly to see if they take flight. If you find that the mother bird is sitting tight withdraw immediately and explain to your children that she might abandon the eggs if frightened. Small children should always be accompanied by an adult on these viewing sessions, and only one child should look at a time. Children soon learn the value of quietness and self-control in this situation.

During incubation only visit the nest once to count the eggs; don't touch them as they are very fragile. You may find there seem to be more fledglings than eggs – this is because the eggs are laid on top of each other and you may not have seen the ones underneath. You will probably be able to hear the fledglings within a few days of hatching, so this is the time to count them. Again, once they emerge nearly ready to fly, watch from a distance or they may be frightened into flying away too early and have less chance of escaping the ever-vigilant predators. Do not try to rescue baby birds fluttering near the nest box. The parent bird may well be nearby, cheeping encouragement from the undergrowth as the

BIRD BOX

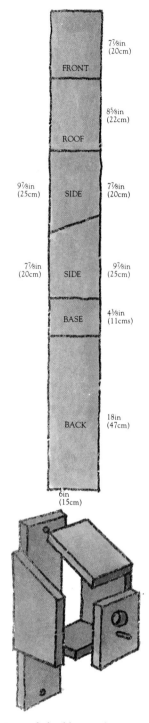

A simple bird box makes a good first carpentry exercise. The wood needs to be painted on the outside only with polyurethane. Position the entry hole ³⁄₄in (20mm) from the top, it should be 1 ¹⁄₈in (28mm) in diameter for a blue tit or tree sparrow. Hinge the roof with a flexible rubber flap, and drill some small holes in the base to let any water drain away.
For further details see addresses on page 172.

fledgling learns to fly.

You may be lucky enough to have more than one clutch in a year in your box; so it is worth giving a weekly check once the first birds have flown. When the box is empty take it down and show the nest to your children. Then clean it out and replace it for next year.

If the box has not been used for three seasons, take it down and position it elsewhere. You may find that birds are nesting naturally in your hedges or bushes – tangled growths of honeysuckle and clematis are particularly popular. Slow-growing evergreens should be trimmed in the autumn to avoid disturbing birds nesting in the spring. For more information see the Bibliography on page 172.

BUTTERFLIES

Butterflies enhance any garden and should be encouraged. They feed on mostly blue and purple flowers, with lots of nectar. They are attracted to plants by smell. Caterpillars feed on the leaves of different plants to the butterflies that develop from them; many of them are usually thought of as weeds.

If you want to plant a butterfly-friendly plot, it should be in a sheltered sunny place. It doesn't have to be very big but the more types of flowering plant you can fit in the most types of butterfly you will attract and for longer, if the plants flower at different times. The centre of this garden could be a purple or white flowering buddleia – not for nothing is this extremely hardy shrub sometimes called the butterfly bush. Butterflies love sweet nectar and a small bowl of syrup and water put out for them in a sunny place will give you a good close-up view of them.

FROGS AND TOADS

If you have a garden pond you will probably find that a frog or toad will appear out of nowhere to breed in it. Frog spawn floats on the surface of the water in a clump while toad spawn is laid in a ribbon shape. It is fascinating to watch the spawn develop. When the tadpoles have their front legs they become carnivorous and feed on insects. If you have them indoors in a tank, feed them on tiny pieces of raw meat.

SNAILS

Snails are among the most accessible wild creatures for children in a garden. Although avid gardeners spend a lot of time trying to eradicate them, they are very interesting for a child to watch. Put some earth and dead leaves into an old square glass fish tank and place it in a spot that is always shadey. Rescue the snails before slug pellets are to be scattered (these pellets are very poisonous and should anyway be used with extreme caution in a family with children and pets) and put them in the tank, covered with a lid pierced with air holes. Supply them daily with fresh leaves that they like – these include hollyhock, calendula, stocks and lovage. Spray the snails with water from a garden spray once a day. Snails shoot their small, round, white eggs out onto the soil, so you may find a crop of baby snails developing. Snails don't object to being lifted out and gently held.

APPENDIX

POISON PLANT CHART

Although many people know about common poisonous plants and berries like deadly nightshade and yew, there are many, many other species of apparently innocuous plants and trees which are poisonous. Some may be weeds, others cultivated in the garden or as house plants. Obviously the most vulnerable age group for poisoning in this way is the under-fives, but this does not mean that older children are immune to the challenges of a dare or may actually mistake a type of berry for something they believe to be edible.

Unfortunately, symptoms of poisoning are rarely evident very soon after a plant has been eaten. The first clue an adult may have is discovering a piece of leaf in a child's hand. Alternatively, a child may complain of a headache, seem exhausted, may vomit or develop an itchy skin. At this point it's worth asking the child whether he has eaten any plants or berries. If he has, the plant needs to be identified as soon as possible to ensure that precautions can be taken if necessary.

If you have reason to believe that your child has eaten something poisonous, call a doctor or go to your nearest hospital Accident and Emergency department. The doctor will get the advice of the poison information centre, or in the USA, call your regional poison control centre.

Then, as calmly as possible, try to find out the answers to the following:

○ What plant the child has eaten
○ Which part of the plant has been eaten and how much
○ When it was eaten
○ If the child has already vomited
○ If at all possible, gather a sample from the plant – a twig, berry and flower, and a bulb or root too if it is above ground and could possibly be the cause. Take a sample of vomit as well if there is one
○ The age of the child is important, have this information to hand when you phone.

If your child eats a plant that you suspect is poisonous and you can't contact a doctor for some hours, you will need to make the child vomit, to insure that as little of the poison is ingested as possible.

NEVER MAKE AN UNCONSCIOUS PERSON VOMIT.

Teach your children at an early age which plants are poisonous; point them out as you see them. As you can see from the list below, it's not just berries that are dangerous.

If there is an established poisonous plant, like a laburnum, in a garden in which your children regularly play, but you can't or don't want to uproot it, make sure they know it's poisonous.

Although some fungi, like wild mushrooms and ceps, are edible, most are not. As it is quite difficult to identify them it is best to leave all varieties well alone, and warn your children to do so as well.

Although every effort has been made to identify poisonous plants, no list like this can ever be complete so make it clear to your children that they should never eat any part of any plant without checking with you first.

It is not always possible to say how much of a particular plant can be fatal, because it depends on many factors such as the age and general physical condition of the child, so always ask the experts.

The illustrations on this page can only act as a guide to identification. Plants can look very similar en masse and a fully mature tree may look very different from a little sapling. It cannot be stressed often enough that medical help must be sought as soon as possible in any case of poisoning.

ALDER BUCKTHORN, BLACK ALDER
(Frangula alnus)
POISONOUS PART Seed, leaf and stem.
SYMPTOMS TO LOOK FOR Vomiting, abdominal pain and diarrhoea.

AMERICAN MISTLETOE
(Phoradendron flavescens)
POISONOUS PART Berries.
SYMPTOMS TO LOOK FOR Gastroenteritis.
CAN BE FATAL

ARNICA (Anica montana)
POISONOUS PART Whole plant.
SYMPTOMS TO LOOK FOR Gastroenteritis, trembling, palpitations of the heart, shortage of breath and cold sweats.
IN EXTREME CASES IT CAN BE FATAL

AUTUMN CROCUS, MEADOW SAFFRON
(Colchicum autumnale)
POISONOUS PART Whole plant.
SYMPTOMS TO LOOK FOR Burning in the mouth, nausea, vomiting, diarrhoea and convulsions.
CAN BE FATAL

AZALEA (Rhododendron)
POISONOUS PART Flowers and leaves.
SYMPTOMS TO LOOK FOR Vomiting, diarrhoea, intestinal cramp and dizziness.

BANEBERRY, HERB CHRISTOPHER (Actaea)
POISONOUS PART Berries.
SYMPTOMS TO LOOK FOR Vomiting, diarrhoea and blisters on the skin.
CAN BE FATAL IN EXTREME CASES

BEAN, COMMON (UNCOOKED)
(Phaseolus vulgaris)
POISONOUS PART Seeds and pods.
SYMPTOMS TO LOOK FOR Nausea, vomiting, stomach pains, diarrhoea and circulatory collapse.
NOTE Heat from cooking destroys the poison.

BEECH (Fagus)
POISONOUS PART Nuts, in large amounts.
SYMPTOMS TO LOOK FOR Abdominal pain, nausea, diarrhoea and in extreme cases convulsions.
CAN BE FATAL IN EXTREME CASES

BLACK BRYONY
(Tamus communis)
POISONOUS PART Berries and root.
SYMPTOMS TO LOOK FOR Burning of the mouth, blistering of the skin, abdominal pain and diarrhoea.
CAN BE FATAL

BLACK LOCUST
(Rubina pseudoa)
POISONOUS PART Inner bark, leaves, seeds

SYMPTOMS TO LOOK FOR
Irritation of mouth and throat, drowsiness, nausea, severe stomach pain, diarrhoea, low blood pressure.

Black Nightshade

BLACK NIGHTSHADE
(Solanum nigrum)
POISONOUS PART Whole plant.
SYMPTOMS TO LOOK FOR Gastric pain, diarrhoea, drowsiness and paralysis after a large dose.

BLUEBELL (Endymion)
POISONOUS PART Bulb.
SYMPTOMS TO LOOK FOR Gastric pain, diarrhoea and blood in the urine.

BUCKTHORN
(Rhamnus catharticus)
POISONOUS PART Berries.
SYMPTOMS TO LOOK FOR Diarrhoea, great thirst and vomiting.

CALICO BUSH (Kalmia)
POISONOUS PART Leaves.
SYMPTOMS TO LOOK FOR Gastric pain, vomiting and breathing difficulties.
CAN BE FATAL

CAPER SPURGE
(Euphorbia lathyris)
POISONOUS PART Whole plant especially the berries.
SYMPTOMS TO LOOK FOR Vomiting and diarrhoea. Can also irritate the skin.

CASTOR OIL PLANT
(Ricinus communis)
POISONOUS PART Seeds or beans.
SYMPTOMS TO LOOK FOR Burning of the mouth, diarrhoea, abdominal pain, weakness and cramps.
CAN BE FATAL

CELANDINE, GREATER, SWALLOW-WORT

(Chelidonium majus)
POISONOUS PART Stem and root.
SYMPTOMS TO LOOK FOR
Burning in the mouth, irritation of the stomach, bloody diarrhoea.

CHALICE VINE, TRUMPET FLOWER

(Solandra guttata)
POISONOUS PART Whole plant.
SYMPTOMS TO LOOK FOR
Hallucinations, headaches, high temperature, weakness and respiratory problems.
CAN BE FATAL

CHERRY LAUREL

(Prunus laurocerasus)
POISONOUS PART Whole plant.
SYMPTOMS TO LOOK FOR
Convulsions and breathing difficulties.
CAN BE FATAL

CHINESE LANTERN

(Physalis alkekengi)
POISONOUS PART Leaves and stem.
SYMPTOMS TO LOOK FOR
Gastroenteritis; urinary problems.

CHOKECHERRY

(Prunus virginiana)
POISONUS PART Berries
SYMPTOMS TO LOOK FOR
Nausea, vomiting

CHRISTMAS CHERRY

(Solanum pseudocapsicum)
POISONOUS PART Berries.
SYMPTOMS TO LOOK FOR
Nausea, abdominal pain and drowsiness.

Christmas Rose

CHRISTMAS ROSE, BLACK HELLEBORE

(Helleborus niger)
POISONOUS PART Whole plant.
SYMPTOMS TO LOOK FOR
Vomiting, diarrhoea, weakness, delirium, convulsion and respiratory failure.
CAN BE FATAL

CLEMATIS

(See Old Man's Beard)

COLUMBINE

(Aquilegia vulgaris)
POISONOUS PART Whole plant.
SYMPTOMS TO LOOK FOR
Mouth and skin tingle, vomiting, diarrhoea, incoordination and respiratory problems.
CAN BE FATAL

CORN COCKLE

(Agrostemma githago)
POISONOUS PART Whole plant.
SYMPTOMS TO LOOK FOR
Vomiting and diarrhoea.
CAN BE FATAL

COWBANE, WATER HEMLOCK (Cicuta virosa)

POISONOUS PART Tuberous rhizome root.
SYMPTOMS TO LOOK FOR
Pains in the mouth, vomiting and convulsions.
CAN BE FATAL

CUCKOO PINT, LORDS AND LADIES (Arum)

POISONOUS PART Leaves and berries.
SYMPTOMS TO LOOK FOR
Vomiting, diarrhoea and weakness.

DAFFODIL (Narcissus)

POISONOUS PART Bulb.
SYMPTOMS TO LOOK FOR
Vomiting, diarrhoea and possible convulsions.

Deadly Nightshade

DEADLY NIGHTSHADE

(Atropa belladonna)
POISONOUS PART Whole plant, especially berries.
SYMPTOMS TO LOOK FOR
Dilatation of pupils, reddening of the face, dry mouth, acceleration of the pulse, fits of frenzy, coma and respiratory paralysis.
CAN BE FATAL

DELPHINIUM (see Larkspur)

DUMBCANE (Dieffenbachia)

POISONOUS PART Stem.
SYMPTOMS TO LOOK FOR
Burning in the mouth, swelling affecting breathing and swallowing.

ELDER (Sambucus nigra)

POISONOUS PART Stem, leaf, root and raw berries.
SYMPTOMS TO LOOK FOR
Vomiting, nausea and diarrhoea, skin can be irritated by berries and leaves.

ELEPHANT'S-EARS

(Caledium vestes)
POISONOUS PART Leaves
SYMPTOMS TO LOOK FOR
Nausea, vomiting, mouth and throat irritation.

FALSE HELLEBORE (Veratrum album)

POISONOUS PART Whole plant.
SYMPTOMS TO LOOK FOR
Burning in the mouth, vomiting, diarrhoea, breathing difficulties, painful muscles and a slow pulse.
CAN BE FATAL

FOOL'S PARSLEY, LESSER HEMLOCK

(Aethusa cynapium)
POISONOUS PART Whole plant.
SYMPTOMS TO LOOK FOR
Vomiting, diarrhoea, mental confusion, trembling, convulsions and coma.

FOUR O'CLOCKS

(Mirabilis Jalapa)
POISONOUS PART Leaves and flowers.
SYMPTOMS TO LOOK FOR
Hallucinations

Foxglove

FOXGLOVE (Digitalis purpurea)

POISONOUS PART Whole plant.
SYMPTOMS TO LOOK FOR
Vomiting, diarrhoea, dizziness, mental disturbance and convulsions.
CAN BE FATAL

GARLAND FLOWER (Daphne cneorum)

POISONOUS PART Whole plant.
SYMPTOMS TO LOOK FOR
Burning in the mouth and stomach, swelling of the face, difficulty in swallowing, nausea, vomiting, diarrhoea and possible muscular twitching.

GLORY LILY, CLIMBING LILY

(Gloriosa)
POISONOUS PART Whole plant.
SYMPTOMS TO LOOK FOR
Diarrhoea, pains in the stomach.
CAN BE FATAL

Hemlock

HEMLOCK (Conium maculatum)

POISONOUS PART Whole plant.
SYMPTOMS TO LOOK FOR
Vomiting, diarrhoea, mental confusion, convulsions, coma and respiratory failure.
CAN BE FATAL

HENBANE (Hyoscyamus)

POISONOUS PART Whole plant.
SYMPTOMS TO LOOK FOR
Dilatation of pupils, reddening of the face, dry mouth, acceleration of the pulse, fits of frenzy, coma and respiratory paralysis.

HERB MERCURY, DOG'S MERCURY

(Mercurialis perennis)
POISONOUS PART Whole plant.
SYMPTOMS TO LOOK FOR
Diarrhoea and severe gastric irritation.

HERB PARIS

(Paris quadrifolia)
POISONOUS PART Whole plant, particularly the berries.
SYMPTOMS TO LOOK FOR
Vomiting, headaches, diarrhoea, and breathing problems.

HOLLY (Ilex aquifolium)

POISONOUS PART Berries.
SYMPTOMS TO LOOK FOR
Vomiting and diarrhoea.
CAN BE FATAL FOR CHILDREN

HONEYSUCKLE (Lonicera)
POISONOUS PART Berries.
SYMPTOMS TO LOOK FOR
Stomach pain.

HYDRANGEA (Hydrangea macrphylla)
POISONOUS PART Flowers and leaves.
SYMPTOMS TO LOOK FOR
Diarrhoea, stomach pain and nausea.

ITALIAN ARUM (Arum italicum)
(See Cuckoo Pint)

IVY (Hedera helix)
POISONOUS PART Leaves, stem and berries.
SYMPTOMS TO LOOK FOR
Vomiting, diarrhoea and burning in the throat.

JACK-IN-THE-PULPIT
(Arisaema triphyllum)
POISONOUS PART Leaves and stem
SYMPTOMS TO LOOK FOR
Nausea, vomiting, throat and mouth irritation

JERUSALEM CHERRY
(Solanum pseudocapsicum)
POISONOUS PART Leaves and berries
SYMPTOMS TO LOOK FOR
Nausea and vomiting

JIMSON WEED, THORN APPLE
(Datura stramonium)
POISONOUS PART Seeds, leaves and berries.
SYMPTOMS TO LOOK FOR
Enlarged pupils, vomiting, great thirst, twitching and convulsions.
CAN BE FATAL

JONQUIL (See Daffodil)

Laburnam

LABURNUM (Laburnum anagyroides)
POISONOUS PART Whole plant, especially seeds.
SYMPTOMS TO LOOK FOR
Vomiting, convulsions, abdominal pains and coma.
CAN BE FATAL

LANTANA (Lantana camara)
POISONOUS PART Berries.
SYMPTOMS TO LOOK FOR
Stomach pains, diarrhoea, weakness.
CAN BE FATAL

Larkspur

LARKSPUR (Delphinium)
POISONOUS PART Seeds and leaves.
SYMPTOMS TO LOOK FOR
Vomiting, nausea, constipation, paralysis, irregular heart beat and breathing difficulties.
CAN BE FATAL

LILY OF THE VALLEY
(Convallaria majalis)
POISONOUS PART Whole plant.
SYMPTOMS TO LOOK FOR
Diarrhoea, vomiting, abdominal pain, slow heart beat.
NOTE: If the flowers are picked, the flower water will be toxic.
FATAL IF TAKEN IN LARGE AMOUNTS

LUPIN (Lupinus)
POISONOUS PART Whole part especially seeds.
SYMPTOMS TO LOOK FOR
Respiratory depression and a slow heart beat.

LAUREL (See Cherry Laurel and Spurge or Wood Laurel)

MANDRAKE (Mandragora)
POISONOUS PART Leaves and root.
SYMPTOMS TO LOOK FOR
Insensitivity to touch, very sleepy which may lead to coma.
CAN BE FATAL

MARSH MARIGOLD (Caltha palustris)
POISONOUS PART Leaves and sap.
SYMPTOMS TO LOOK FOR
Burning mouth, stomach pains and skin irritation.

MAY APPLE (Podophyllum peltatum)
POISONOUS PART Root.
SYMPTOMS TO LOOK FOR
Vomiting and diarrhoea.

MAY LILY (Maianthemum)
POISONOUS PART Whole plant, especially the berries.
SYMPTOMS NOT RECORDED

MEZEREON (Daphne mezereum)
POISONOUS PART Sap and berries.
SYMPTOMS TO LOOK FOR
Burning sensation in the mouth, lots of salivar with difficulties in swallowing, the face swells up and there are pains in the stomach and the head and bloody diarrhoea.
CAN BE FATAL

MISTLETOE (Viscum album)
POISONOUS PART Berries.
SYMPTOMS TO LOOK FOR
Stomach ache.

Monks Hood

MONKSHOOD (Aconitum napellus)
POISONOUS PART Whole plant, especially the seeds, leaves and root.
SYMPTOMS TO LOOK FOR
Immediate burning and tingling in the mouth, fingers and toes, numbness, vomiting, diarrhoea, convulsions and breathing becomes very difficult.
NOTE: The poison acts very fast.
CAN BE FATAL

MORNING-GLORY (Ipomoea purpurea)
POISONOUS PART Seeds.
SYMPTOMS TO LOOK FOR
Over-sensitive sense of vision, smell and hearing, can cause brain damage.
CAN BE FATAL

MOUNTAIN LAUREL
(Kalmia latifolia)
POISONOUS PART Leaves
SYMPTOMS TO LOOK FOR
Nausea, vomiting and diarrhoea

NARCISSUS (See Daffodil)

OLD MAN'S BEARD (Clematis vitalba)
POISONOUS PART Whole plant.
SYMPTOMS TO LOOK FOR
Diarrhoea, stomach ache and sores on the skin.
CAN BE FATAL

OLEANDER (Nerium oleander)
POISONOUS PART Whole plant.
SYMPTOMS TO LOOK FOR
Drowsiness, vomiting, diarrhoea, stomach ache, breathing difficulties and coma.
NOTE: The poison acts very fast.
CAN BE FATAL

OPIUM POPPY (Papaver somniferum)
POISONOUS PART Whole plant, especially the unripe seed capsules.
SYMPTOMS TO LOOK FOR
Hallucination, headache, dizziness, vomiting, weakness, sleepiness, thirst, very small pupils, slow, irregular breathing.

PASQUE FLOWER (Pulsatilla)
POISONOUS PART Leaves, sap.
SYMPTOMS TO LOOK FOR
Stomach ache and itchy skin.

PHILODENDRON (Sweetheart plant)
POISONOUS PART Leaves
SYMPTOMS TO LOOK FOR
Nausea, vomiting, mouth and throat irritation

POINSETTIA (Euphorbia)
POISONOUS PART Leaves and flowers.
SYMPTOMS TO LOOK FOR
Vomiting, diarrhoea, possible hallucinations and inflammations of the skin.

Poison Ivy

POISON IVY
(Toxicodendron radicans)
POISONOUS PART Whole plant.
SYMPTOMS TO LOOK FOR
Skin blistering, itching.

POISON SUMAC
(Rhus vernix)
See POISON IVY

Poke Weed

POKEWEED, PIGEON BERRY

(Phytolacca decandra)
POISONOUS PART Whole plant.
SYMPTOMS TO LOOK FOR Vomiting, diarrhoea, cramp, difficulties with vision and breathing.
CAN BE FATAL IN INFANTS, OR LARGE DOSES

POPPY (Papaver)
CORN (Papaver rhoeas)
ICELAND (Papaver nudicaule)
POISONOUS PART Whole plant.
SYMPTOMS TO LOOK FOR Drowsiness and a stomach ache.

POTATO (Solanum tuberosum)
POISONOUS PART Leaves, green sprouting tubers and stem.
SYMPTOMS TO LOOK FOR Breathing difficulties and stomach ache.
CAN BE FATAL

POTHOS (Epipremum aureum)
POISONOUS PART Leaves
SYMPTOMS TO LOOK FOR Nausea, vomiting, mouth and throat irritation.

PRIVET (Ligustrum)
POISONOUS PART Berries.
SYMPTOMS TO LOOK FOR Vomiting, diarrhoea.
NOTE: A trimmed privet hedge doesn't have berries.

RAGWORT, BENWEED

(Senecio jacobaea)
POISONOUS PART Whole plant, especially the seeds.
SYMPTOMS TO LOOK FOR Loss of appetite, constipation in short term, could cause liver problems later.

RED BANEBERRY (Actaea)
POISONOUS PART Root, fruit and sap.
SYMPTOMS TO LOOK FOR Vomiting, diarrhoea and dizziness.
CAN BE FATAL

RHODODENDRON (All types)
POISONOUS PART Flowers and leaves.
SYMPTOMS TO LOOK FOR Vomiting, stomach cramp, dizziness and diarrhoea.

RHUBARB (Rheum rhaponticum)
POISONOUS PART Leaves.
SYMPTOMS TO LOOK FOR Vomiting, stomach pain, weakness and diarrhoea.
CAN BE FATAL

ROBINIA (Robinia pseudoacacia)
POISONOUS PART Whole plant, especially the seeds.
SYMPTOMS TO LOOK FOR Vomiting, diarrhoea and difficulty in breathing.

RUE (Ruta graveolens)
POISONOUS PART Leaves and sap.
SYMPTOMS TO LOOK FOR Diarrhoea, and sensitivity to light.

SKUNK CABBAGE

(Symplocarpus foetida)
POISONOUS PART Leaves
SYMPTOMS TO LOOK FOR Nausea, vomiting, mouth and throat irritation

St. JOHN'S WORT

(Hypericum perforatum)
POISONOUS PART Flowers and leaves.
SYMPTOMS TO LOOK FOR Not recorded.

SNOWBERRY (Symphoricarpos)
POISONOUS PART Berries.
SYMPTOMS TO LOOK FOR Vomiting, diarrhoea, and can be irritating to the skin.

SNOWDROP (Galanthus)
POISONOUS PART Bulb.
SYMPTOMS TO LOOK FOR Vomiting and diarrhoea.

SOLOMON'S SEAL

(Polygonatum)
POISONOUS PART Berries.
SYMPTOMS TO LOOK FOR Vomiting and diarrhoea.

SPINDLE TREE (Euonymus)
POISONOUS PART Leaves, berries and bark.
SYMPTOMS TO LOOK FOR Vomiting, diarrhoea and later unconsciousness.

SPURGE OR WOOD LAUREL

(Daphne laureola)
POISONOUS PART Whole plant especially the berries.
SYMPTOMS TO LOOK FOR Burning in the mouth, swelling of the tongue and lips, vomiting, diarrhoea and delirium.
CAN BE FATAL

SPURGE
CAPER (Euphorbia lathyris)
PETTY (Euphorbia peplus)
SUN, WARTWORT
(Euphorbia helioscopia)
POISONOUS PART Whole plant.
SYMPTOMS TO LOOK FOR Vomiting and diarrhoea. Skin irritation.

STAR OF BETHLEHEM

(Ornithogalum umbellatum)
POISONOUS PART Whole plant.
SYMPTOMS TO LOOK FOR Nausea, stomach ache.

STINKING HELLEBORE

(Helleborus foetidus)
POISONOUS PART Whole plant.
SYMPTOMS TO LOOK FOR Vomiting, diarrhoea, delirium, convulsions, respiratory failure.
CAN BE FATAL

STINKING IRIS (Iris)
POISONOUS PART Whole plant, especially berries.
SYMPTOMS TO LOOK FOR Gastroenteritis.

TOBACCO (Nicotiana tabacum)
POISONOUS PART Leaves.
SYMPTOMS TO LOOK FOR See Hemlock.
NOTE: Nicotine is easily absorbed through the skin.
CAN BE FATAL

TOMATO

(Lycopersicum esculentum)
POISONOUS PART Leaves and stem.
SYMPTOMS TO LOOK FOR See Woody Nightshade.

VIBURNUM, GUELDA ROSE

(Viburnum opulus)
POISONOUS PART Berries, bark and leaves.
SYMPTOMS TO LOOK FOR Vomiting, diarrhoea.
CAN BE FATAL

VIRGINIA CREEPER

(Parthenocissus)
POISONOUS PART Leaves, berries.
SYMPTOMS TO LOOK FOR Gastroenteritis, irritation to mouth and throat.

WATER DROPWORT
WATER HEMLOCK

(Oenanthe)
POISONOUS PART Whole plant.
SYMPTOMS TO LOOK FOR Enlarged pupils, salivation and convulsions.
CAN BE FATAL

WHITE BRYONY (Bryonia)
POISONOUS PART Whole plant, especially berries.
SYMPTOMS TO LOOK FOR Vomiting and diarrhoea.

WHITE HELLEBORE (Veratrum viride)
POISONOUS PART Whole plant.
SYMPTOMS TO LOOK FOR Headache, difficulties in breathing, some salivation and possible hallucinations.

WISTERIA, JAPANESE AND CHINESE

(Wisteria floribunda and sisensis)
POISONOUS PART Seeds and berries.
SYMPTOMS TO LOOK FOR Vomiting, diarrhoea, stomach pain and dehydration.

WOOD ANEMONE (Anemone nemorosa)
POISONOUS PART Leaves and sap.
SYMPTOMS TO LOOK FOR Dizziness, problems with circulation and breathing, short term.

WOODY NIGHTSHADE

(Solanum dulcamara) (See Black Nightshade)

YELLOW JESSAMINE

(Gelsemium sempervirens)
POISONOUS PART Flowers, berries and stem.
SYMPTOMS TO LOOK FOR Double vision, weakness, respiratory problems.
CAN BE FATAL

Yew

YEW (Taxus baccata)
POISONOUS PART Leaves and seeds.
SYMPTOMS TO LOOK FOR Dizziness, vomiting, diarrhoea, dilatation of the pupils, reddening of the lips and respiratory paralysis.
CAN BE FATAL

DOMESTIC PETS

This chart is simply a guide to the impact a particular animal may have on the family home. For details of choosing and caring for your chosen pet, consult a specialist publication or veterinary surgeon. It is fun for the children to help choose an animal.

It's important to give careful thought to what pet suits your family before your child sets her heart on an unsuitable animal. For instance, unless there is someone at home for a large part of the day, every day, and probably will be for the next ten to fourteen years, a dog isn't the answer.

If you have pets before the children are born, the children will have to fit in with them, unless they could in some way be a danger to them, in which case the animals should be found new homes. If, however, you have no pets, but would like one, wait until your children are old enough not to pull its tail or be frightened by it.

Animals are a tie – if your children are under ten, the chances are you will be doing most of the caring, and if they are older, you will probably find the pet remains with you in five or six years time when your children leave home, so it helps if you are happy with the pet too.

BIRDS Birds generally prefer to be kept in pairs as they like company. The cage needs to be the right one for that particular species and needs to be relined every two days and scrubbed every two weeks. The floor beneath the cage tends to be littered with feathers and pieces of broken seed.
LIFE EXPECTANCY of a few examples. BUDGERIGARS usually 6–8 years or much longer. COCKATOOS 25–45 years, or up to 90. PARROTS Depending on the species, 20–70 years

CATS These are good pets for a town-based family. A pet door gives them the independence they enjoy. If your home may be empty for a large part of the day in the future, when your children are at school, it is kinder to have two cats, to keep each other company. Unless trained to do otherwise, cats will scratch the furniture and carpets, so give them a scratching pole and encourage them to use it. Keep the door closed on rooms that have precious furniture in them. A litter of kittens is lovely for children to experience but you need to be confident that you can find good homes for them. Long haired cats need daily brushing.
LIFE EXPECTANCY 16–20 years

DOGS Talk to a vet about what breed would be suitable for your family. Dogs need walking three times a day, and lots of company, but a really good walk during the winter means a lot of mud. It is worth finding a special place where your dog can dry off before coming into the main living areas (see utility rooms p. 51). Long haired dogs need daily grooming and leave hairs around. Poodle fur is non-allergenic to most asthma sufferers. A large or exuberant dog can be very frightening for a child who may only be about the same height.
LIFE EXPECTANCY 14–16 years

FISH Cold water fish need cleaning out about twice a week and should live in a tank rather than a bowl. Tropical fish need a filtration system, which should be cleaned out once a

week, and glass and large stones in the tank should be cleaned without emptying the tank itself.
LIFE EXPECTANCY About 5 years

GERBILS These like to live in pairs of the same sex, unless you want to breed them. They can live in cages or an aquarium with sand to burrow in, with additional nesting material. This keeps the bedding well contained. The aquarium should have a lid with air holes to protect them from any cats. If they are kept in a cage the sawdust and bedding tends to end up all around the cage; you can catch most of it if you put the cage in a deep sided tray, like a cat litter tray. Gerbils are best not kept in the bedroom because of the noise they make at night.
LIFE EXPECTANCY About 5 years

GUINEA PIGS Cuddly animals, these live in a hutch outside in the summer, but need to have a space inside during the winter. They can live in pairs or separately, and sit very still when they are picked up so are therefore good to hug.
LIFE EXPECTANCY About 5 years

HAMSTERS are nocturnal, which is not a bad thing because by the time your children are old enough to look after them they will be at school for a lot of the day. They are usually very friendly to people but have to live in a cage by themselves, so if you want to breed them you will need space for more than one cage. Like most rodents, they can give a nasty nip, but are usually good-tempered. They spread their bedding and food outside the cage and are noisy at night.
LIFE EXPECTANCY About 3 years

MICE/RATS These have a strong smell so they have to be cleaned out twice a week. They live in pairs happily, and breed very easily, so aim to buy the same sex. Domestic female rats smell less than males and are rather intelligent. Mice can squeeze through incredibly small holes.
LIFE EXPECTANCY Up to 3 years

RABBITS Rabbits which are used to being handled when young are best, so try to buy young rabbits rather than adults. Choose a breed that is known to be good for children to handle. Two females live together happily but two males fight. A female rabbit and a guinea pig can co-habit as well. Rabbits are kept out all year, so long as this is what they have always been used to, and the hutch is in a sheltered place out of the wind.
LIFE EXPECTANCY 6–8 years

SNAKES AND LIZARDS These don't make good domestic family pets. They often escape, and they have to be fed on live or very recently killed food and the aquarium needs to be cleaned scrupulously every three weeks.
LIFE EXPECTANCY Depending on size, 10–20 years

TERRAPINS AND TURTLES These are the domestic pets most often offered to zoos, because they live a long time and grow very large, so need a large heated aquarium. This needs frequent cleaning which is hard because of the size. They may also carry the salmonella virus.
LIFE EXPECTANCY 20 years

STAIN REMOVAL

Deal with the stain as quickly as possible. Make sure your children tell you when they have spilt something; promise not to be cross – and don't be.

ALWAYS CHECK FOR COLOUR FASTNESS FIRST ON A SMALL AREA THAT CAN'T BE SEEN.

Because some dyes and fabrics don't react as you would expect them to, use a white cotton cloth or white kitchen towel to clear up the spill to ensure that what is stained has no dye in it that runs.

Never smoke when solvents are being used. When removing a stain, dab it, don't rub it; work from the outside inwards, otherwise you will spread the stain.

With any stain, soak up any excess fluid by pressing or standing on kitchen towel until it is all absorbed. Any solid deposits need to be removed before the stain is dealt with.

UPHOLSTERY Be careful not to wet the stain too much; keep blotting with a towel as you work. If the stain is on a delicate fabric or if you are in any way worried call professional help, but it has to be called immediately or the expert may not be able to help you.

CARPET Again, don't saturate the stain. Water soluble stains can be removed with a carpet shampoo or 'trouble shooter'. You may need to shampoo the whole carpet afterwards. 'Stain Devils' are not suitable for rubber backed carpets.

Keep a stain removal kit, containing the following: a range of Stain Devils, a soda syphon (club soda), glycerine, methylated spirit (rubbing alcohol), carpet shampoo trouble shooter, white spirit (white gasoline), white vinegar and a bottle of dry cleaning spot remover.

TREATMENT FOR CARPETS AND UPHOLSTERY

ADHESIVE Use childrens' adhesives where ever possible, they are washable, even model making glues. If however an adhesive has been spilt that isn't washable scrape up all the excess on a knife, taking care not to spread it. Use the manufacturer's solvent if at all possible, or water; keep it wet until you have managed to pick out as much as possible without damaging the fabric.

ALCOHOLIC SPIRITS Soak up as much as possible, then squirt with soda water (club soda) or dab with a warm damp cloth, shampoo if necessary. If the stain is old try methylated spirit (rubbing alcohol) to reduce it.

BALL-POINT Methylated spirit (rubbing alcohol) removes most ball-point inks, if you act fast enough, or try dabbing with lukewarm water.

BEER Blot well; if the stain is fresh, squirt sparingly with soda water, then treat with biological detergent or carpet and upholstery trouble shooter. If it is dry, dab it with methylated spirits (rubbing alcohol), or the appropriate Stain Devil.

BLOOD If the stain is fresh, squirt with soda water or a little cold salt water. If the stain is dry try a solution of biological detergent.

CHEWING GUM Remove as much as possible, taking care not to push it further into the fibres. Use the appropriate Stain Devil or freeze with an ice pack for about an hour, break off as much as you can and treat the rest with methylated spirit (rubbing alcohol), white spirit (white gasoline) or paint brush cleaner.

CHOCOLATE Scrape up all the excess on a knife blade, pour a small amount of glycerine onto the stain, and leave for a while to moisten, then dab it with lukewarm water and pure soap. Rinse with clear water. Alternatively use the Stain Devil for the purpose.

COFFEE Soak up as much liquid as possible and squirt with soda water (club soda) or dab with warm water, then use a carpet trouble shooter, dry cleaning fluid or Stain Devil.

CURRY Soak up any liquid and apply glycerine immediately to stop it drying out, leave it for about ten minutes then dab with warm water and rinse. If it is a large mark it may need to be professionally treated.

EGG Scrape up as much as possible on the blade of a knife, without spreading it, dab on dry cleaning fluid or a carpet trouble shooter.

EXCRETA Remove it from the carpet or upholstery, wiping up as much as possible with tissue, being careful not to rub the fabric, then shampoo with carpet shampoo or trouble shooter.

FATS OR OILS Dab on dry cleaning fluid, or the relevent Stain Devil.

FELT TIP Dab with water and washing up liquid if they are washable; if not use methylated spirit (rubbing alcohol) carefully so the stain doesn't spread.

FRUIT JUICE Soak up as much as possible with kitchen towel, then shampoo with carpet shampoo and if there are any traces left dab them with methylated spirit (rubbing alcohol).

ICE CREAM Remove as much as possible and dab with warm water unless it is chocolate or fruit flavour in which case, treat as recommended for them.

INK Blot with salt immediately, when it has soaked up as much as it is going to, vacuum or gently brush it off, so that you don't spread the stain. Then dab carefully with lemon juice, and finally shampoo or spray with a carpet spot remover.

JAM AND MARMALADE Scrape up as much as possible and wipe up with lukewarm water, or methylated spirit (rubbing alcohol).

KETCHUP Same as JAM AND MARMALADE.

LIPSTICK Scrape excess off with a knife and remove the rest with paint brush cleaner or carpet spot remover. If it is on upholstery dab with eucalyptus oil or dry cleaning fluid.

MILK Soak up as much as possible, squirt with soda water or dab with lukewarm water. Because any milk left behind will smell it's important to flush it out well, but be sure to blot it as you work, then shampoo or treat with the trouble shooter.

MUD Let the mud dry completely then vacuum it up.

PAINTS, CHILDREN'S WATER-BASED Scrape up any excess taking great care not to spread it, dab with cold water and some washing up liquid. Purple, black and (surprisingly) yellow can be particularly difficult. If this fails dab with a little undiluted household ammonia then rinse thoroughly.

PAINT, OIL-BASED (GLOSS) Scrape up any excess paint on the blade of a knife being careful not to spread it, and dab with paintbrush cleaner.

PAINT, WATER-BASED Scrape any excess off on the blade of a knife and sponge with cold water immediately, or dab with a brush cleaner.

PLASTICINE AND FIMO (MODELLING CLAY) Pick off as much as possible and then treat the remainder with dry cleaning fluid.

SHOE POLISH Scrape off as much as possible on the blade of a knife and dab with white spirit (white gasoline), then shampoo.

SOFT DRINKS Soak up any liquid and dab with cold water and washing up liquid. If the stain hasn't disappeared treat with a solution of methylated spirits (rubbing alcohol) with a little white vinegar added to it.

TEA Soak up as much as possible on some kitchen towel and sponge with warm water. If you have some glycerine it's easier to get the stain out if you put it on the stain the moment it is spilt, then shampoo it out. If the stain is old add glycerine and leave it for a few hours and then shampoo out.

URINE Soak up as much as possible on some kitchen towel, give it a quick squirt with soda water or cold water and then shampoo.

VOMIT Scrape up the vomit with a spoon and blot the area, then shampoo the area with a few drops of disinfectant in the water.

WINE Red wine: blot well, pour enough white wine on it to wet it, blot it again and it should be gone. If not use carpet shampoo or Stain Devil. White wine doesn't stain so blot it well and wipe with warm water to get rid of any smell or stickyness.

WALLS

Finger marks can easily be wiped off vinyl emulsion, gloss paint and most wallpapers. If the wallpaper isn't washable a wadge of fresh bread cleans off some marks.

WAX CRAYON AND PENCIL Use an eraser, on a hidden area try rubbing firmly rather than gingerly.

FELT-TIP PEN As the ink varies you will need to try several methods on another area before you treat the stain. Washable pens designed especially for children's use should only need a wipe with a damp soapy cloth, if this doesn't work, try lighter fuel, or methylated spirit (rubbing alcohol).

HEIGHT AND REACH CHART

BOYS

AGE	HEIGHT	REACH IN INCHES
1	30	37
2	34	41
3	37	47
4	40	51
5	42½	54½
6	45	58
7	47½	61½
8	50	64½
9	51½	68
10	54	70½
11	56	74
12	57½	76½
13	60	78½
14	63	81
15	66½	85
16	68	87
17	68½	88
18	69	88½
19	69	88½

AGE	HEIGHT	REACH IN CMS
1	76	94
2	85	104
3	94	119
4	101	129
5	108	138
6	114	147
7	120	156
8	126	164
9	131	172
10	136	179
11	141	188
12	146	194
13	152	199
14	160	206
15	168	215
16	172	221
17	173	224
18	174	225
19	174	225

This chart is designed to help you position locks, switches, spy holes, shelves etc around your home so that they can be used by a child when you feel they are old enough, and alternatively to keep things out of reach of those you think are too young. The measurements in the chart are only approximate; they are worked out on the average height of a child on a particular birthday. If your children are tall or small for their age you should take this into account.

GIRLS

AGE	HEIGHT	REACH IN INCHES
1	29	35½
2	33½	41
3	36½	45
4	39½	50
5	42	54
6	44½	57
7	47	60
8	49	63
9	51	66
10	53½	70
11	55½	73½
12	59	77
13	62	82
14	63	83
15	64	84½
16	64	85

AGE	HEIGHT	REACH IN CMS
1	74	90
2	84	104
3	93	115
4	100	126
5	107	137
6	113	145
7	119	152
8	125	160
9	130	168
10	136	177
11	142	186
12	150	196
13	157	208
14	160	213
15	162	214
16	162	216

Children can reach higher than you think and younger children can be quite determined and resourceful when they want to be. An older child likes to be independent and it's in everybody's best interest if they can help themselves to what they need over the age of about five, but you will know when your own child is ready.

CONCLUSION

If you live the kind of life where, after a sleep-interrupted night with the baby, you have to eat your toast while you are packing a lunch box, so that you can put the washing on before getting the children off to school and the baby to the babysitter, leaving your home looking the way you would like to come back to it later, and still have time for a spot of power walking before starting work, then you will have understood the point of this book. Nowhere are time and motion more important than in a family home. When the mundane areas are established, style is easier to achieve.

Writing this book has made me think much harder about good use of space in the home. It is too easy to waste space and to become accustomed to inconveniences without really noticing them. When there are children in a home, space is one of the most precious commodities, so finding better ways of using it, with an eye to the future as well, could make all our lives a lot more comfortable.

Watch the way your children use their surroundings and change them if there is an obvious need to. For instance, if you have to drop to your knees with a cloth every time someone walks into your home, or live with footprints until you have time and energy to do something about them, or if you have to straighten the rug every time you walk past it, it shows that you have two problems: one is irritation, the other safety.

Having to clear up all the time after your children and their friends leads to resentment. You should be able to welcome other children into your home without worrying about the dirt and devastation, and although there is inevitably some friction about tidying up, if you have thought about making it as easy as possible everyone will be more co-operative. But don't let it wait – act now to get rid of that irritating or potentially dangerous problem and you'll wonder why you didn't do it months ago.

It is as well not to be too ambitious and try to change too much at any one time. Large projects are especially difficult with babies and young children in the home; it will be counter-productive if you end up having to live in a building site with a young family – this is both dangerous and wearing so take it step by step. A well-designed home should be flexible enough to accommodate everyone's needs, and if you refer to the ideas in the preceding pages as your children grow up, everyone can benefit.

We are all more influenced by our surroundings than we probably realize and our environment can have the power either to increase levels of stress or to relax us. The aim of a well-designed house is to reduce some of the practical, everyday stresses and enable those of us who have or are about to have children to live together as harmoniously as possible.

The design of this delightful room demonstrates a good sense of colour and a lot of confidence. The castle in the middle of the room stands on a low cupboard that holds toys and any extra furniture from the palace above. The corner seat has three uses, as a seat, a cupboard and a step up to reach the shelves. The raspberries-and-cream pink floor has been created by combining white floor paint with a just a touch of red. The rainbow theme in the curtains is echoed on the walls, the floor and the ceiling.

ADDRESSES
& BIBLIOGRAPHY

ADDRESSES IN THE UK

ACTIVITY TOYS
TUBE PLASTIC LTD
SEVERN ROAD
STOURPORT-ON-
SEVERN
WORCS
Tel (0299) 827728
(Garden toys)

THE BRITISH TRUST
FOR ORNITHOLOGY
BEECH GROVE
TRING
HERTFORDSHIRE
HP23 5NR
(Bird tables and boxes)

CROWN BERGER
EUROPE LTD
PO BOX 37
CROWN HOUSE
HOLLINS ROAD
DARWEN
LANCASHIRE
BB3 0BG

ELECTRAK
INTERNATIONAL LTD
45 HIGH STREET
KINGSTON-UPON-
THAMES
SURREY
KT1 1LQ
Tel (081) 547 2121
(Childproof sockets)

ELFA STORAGE SYSTEMS
DOMESTIC STORAGE
SYSTEMS LTD
YSTRAD MYNACH
MID GLAMORGAN
Tel (0443) 814831

FULDA CARPET STOP
BRYAN AND CLARK
BROS. LTD
KERN HOUSE
SCRUBS LANE
LONDON NW10 6QX
Tel (081) 969 9933
(Carpet underfelt)

HABITAT DESIGNS LTD
HITHERCROFT ROAD
WALLINGFORD
OXON
OX10 9EU
Tel (0491) 35000

HAGO PRODUCTS LTD
SHRIPNEY ROAD
BOGNOR REGIS
WEST SUSSEX
PO22 9NH
Tel (0243) 863131
(Childproofing equipment)

HUDVAD
HUDVAD HOUSE
130–132 TERRACE ROAD
WALTON-ON-THAMES
SURREY
KT12 2EA
Tel (0932) 247835
(Central heating radiators)

IKEA INCORPORATED
SERVICE OFFICE
225 NORTH CIRCULAR
ROAD
LONDON NW10 0JQ
Tel (071) 451 2813

MAMAS & PAPAS
QUEENS MILL ESTATE
QUEENS MILL ROAD
HUDDERSFIELD
HD1 3RR
WEST YORKS
Tel (0484) 512471
(Baby equipment)

NATIONAL PLAYING
FIELDS ASSOCIATION
25 OVINGTON SQUARE
LONDON SW3 1LQ
Tel (081) 584 6445
(Information for play
surfaces)

PAINT
MANUFACTURERS
ASSOCIATION
ALEMBIC HOUSE
93 ALBERT
EMBANKMENT
LONDON
SE1 7TY
Tel (071) 582 1185

THE TREE COUNCIL
35 BELGRAVE SQUARE
LONDON SW1X 8QN
Tel (071) 235 8854

ADDRESSES IN NORTH AMERICA

A-PLUS PRODUCTS INC.
PO BOX 4057
SANTA MONICA
CALIFORNIA 90404
Tel (213) 399 1177
(Baby products)

BADGER BASKET
COMPANY
616 NORTH COURT
SUITE 150
PALATINE
ILLINOIS 60067
(Bassinettes and furniture)
Tel (312) 991 3800

ELFA CORPORATION OF
AMERICA
PO BOX 3346
PRINCETOWN
NEW JERSEY 08543
Tel (609) 920 0007

HUDVAD (CANADA)
2408 10th AVENUE
S.W. CALGARY
ALBERTA T 3C 0KX
Tel (403) 249 7740

IKEA INCORPORATED
SERVICE OFFICE
PLYMOUTH COMMONS
BUILDINGS
PLYMOUTH MEETING
PA 19462
Tel (215) 834 0180

JUVENILE PRODUCTS
MANUFACTURERS
ASSOCIATION
66 EAST MAIN ST.
MOORSTOWN
NJ 08057
Tel (609) 234 9155

NATIONAL SPA AND
POOL INSTITUTE
2111 ISENHOWER
AVENUE
ALEXANDRA
VIRGINIA 22314
Tel (703) 838 0083

Below is a list of specialist books which goes into more detail on specific subjects than I have been able to in the previous pages.

BETTER HOMES AND GARDENS Your floors and stairs (Meredith)
BRYAN, FELICITY A garden for children (Michael Joseph)
BURKE, KEN How to attract birds (Ortho Books)
DAVIES, KEELING & TROWBRIDGE Fantasy finishes (Macdonald Orbis)
EFFRON, EDWARD Planning and designing lighting (Windward)
GLUE, DAVID The garden bird book (British Trust for Ornithology)
GRAY & INNES Decorating techniques (Orbis)

DU FEU, CHRIS Nestboxes (BTO)
JOHNSON, LORRAINE The new decorator's directory (Mermaid Books)
KRESS, STEPHEN The Audubon Society guide to attracting birds (Scribners)
METZGER & WHITTAKER The childproofing check list (Doubleday)
PROCTOR, DR NOBLE Garden birds (Rodale Books)
PURVES, LIBBY How not to be a perfect mother (Fontana)
SAYER, SU Playing safe (Thorsons)
WILHIDE & SPENCER Low cost high style (Conran Octopus)

INDEX

ACKNOWLEDGEMENTS

PHOTOGRAPHIC CREDITS

P.1 DI LEWIS/EWA
P.2 PIERS BIZONY/RICHARD VANSPALL
P.6 PIERS BIZONY/RICHARD VANSPALL
P.7 KARL-DIETRICH BUHLER/EWA
P.9 PIERS BIZONY/RICHARD VANSPALL
P.10 PIERS BIZONY/RICHARD VANSPALL
P.11 JON BOUCHIER/EWA
P.12/13 RODNEY HYETT/EWA
P.14 HAGO Top left
    IKEA Top right
    IKEA Bottom right
P.16 CROWN/BERGER
P.17 PIERS BIZONY/RICHARD VANSPALL
P.18 CLIVE HELM/EWA
P.19 EDWARD EFFRON
P.22 EWA Top left
P.22 EWA Top right
    PIERS BIZONY/RICHARD VANSPALL Bottom
P.23 PIERS BIZONY/RICHARD VANSPALL
P.24 PIERS BIZONY/RICHARD VANSPALL
P.25 PIERS BIZONY/RICHARD VANSPALL
P.27 PIERS BIZONY/RICHARD VANSPALL
P.28 PIERS BIZONY/RICHARD VANSPALL
P.29 PIERS BIZONY/RICHARD VANSPALL
P.30 HABITAT (both)
P.31 PIERS BIZONY/RICHARD VANSPALL
P.32 TOM LEIGHTON/EWA
P.32/33 TOM LEIGHTON/EWA
P.34/35 PIERS BIZONY/RICHARD VANSPALL
P.36 IKEA
P.37 EMILY HOLT
P.39 PIERS BIZONY/RICHARD VANSPALL
P.40 IKEA (both)
P.41 HAGO
P.42 RODNEY HYETT/EWA
P.44/45 PIERS BIZONY/RICHARD VANSPALL
P.46 IKEA
P.47 SPIKE POWELL/EWA
P.50 ELFA
P.51 IKEA
P.52 MICHAEL DUNNE/EWA
P.53 MICHAEL DUNNE/EWA
P.57 PIERS BIZONY/RICHARD VANSPALL
P.58 PIERS BIZONY/RICHARD VANSPALL

I would like to thank Alice and George Bird, Jago Brown, Sophie Cox, Roger Diski, Cherry and Mike Doyle, Lisa Eveleigh, Dr Briony Fer, Gillian and Stephen Gilbert, Harriet Griffey, Hammersmith, Renny Harrop, Becky and Katie Herbert, Emily and Polly Holt, Charlie and Flora King, Jessica Mauntner, Granger McCallin, Hilary and Charles McCallin, Bertie Mitchell, Yasmin Quadir, John Robertson, Liz and Tim Ross, Brie Rogers Lowery, Pat and Howard Sheldon, Angela Southon, Polly and Daisy Staniford, Anella Wickenden, D.A.C.O. White, Carol Wooley Hill.

DESIGNERS

Judy Bird, June and Bryn Bird, Fenella and Michael Brown, Jane and Charles Cook, Beatriz Echeverri and Patrick Wakely, Jenny and Nick Evans, Jane and Geoffrey Gibberd, Anne and John Holt, Janey and Caradoc King, Melanie and Clive Langer, Tanya McCallin and Michael Blakemore, Doreen Mitchell, Gill and Ian Pryce, Debbie and Mike Staniford, Carol and Phillip Thomas, Karen and Lawrence Wright.

Illustrations by Caroline and John Astrop are on pages 5, 13, 20/21, 43, 48, 54, 55, 56, 67, 71, 76/77, 99, 100, 106, 114, 136, 137, 145, 158–167.

Architectural drawings by Hilary Davies are on pages 113, 115, 120, 128.

P.59 PIERS BIZONY/RICHARD VANSPALL
P.61 PIERS BIZONY/RICHARD VANSPALL
P.62/63 PIERS BIZONY/RICHARD VANSPALL
P.64 MICHAEL DUNNE/EWA
P.65 HAGO
P.66 SPIKE POWELL/EWA
P.68 PIERS BIZONY/RICHARD VANSPALL
P.69 ELFA
P.70 EDWARD EFFRON
P.71 MICHAEL DUNNE/EWA
P.72 PIERS BIZONY/RICHARD VANSPALL
P.73 PIERS BIZONY/RICHARD VANSPALL
P.74 IKEA
P.75 PIERS BIZONY/RICHARD VANSPALL
P.78 MICHAEL DUNNE/EWA
P.79 MICHAEL DUNNE/EWA
P.80 IKEA
P.81 MICHAEL DUNNE/EWA
P.82 ELFA (both)
P.83 IKEA
P.84 PIERS BIZONY/RICHARD VANSPALL
P.85 PIERS BIZONY/RICHARD VANSPALL
P.87 PIERS BIZONY/

RICHARD VANSPALL
P.88 EWA
P.89 PIERS BIZONY/RICHARD VANSPALL
P.90 PIERS BIZONY/RICHARD VANSPALL
P.91 HABITAT
P.92 FRIEDHELM THOMAS/EWA
P.93 HUDVAD
P.94 PIERS BIZONY/RICHARD VANSPALL
P.96 NEIL LORIMER/EWA
P.98 MAMAS & PAPAS (three)
P.101 PIERS BIZONY/RICHARD VANSPALL
P.102 MICHAEL NICHOLSON/EWA
P.103 MICHAEL DUNNE © FRANCIS LINCOLN
P.104 MICHAEL DUNNE/EWA
P.105 PIERS BIZONY/RICHARD VANSPALL
P.107 PIERS BIZONY/RICHARD VANSPALL
P.108 MICHAEL DUNNE/EWA
P.109 MICHAEL NICHOLSON/EWA
P.110 JUDITH ROBERTSON

P.111 PIERS BIZONY/RICHARD VANSPALL
P.112 PIERS BIZONY/RICHARD VANSPALL
P.116 PIERS BIZONY/RICHARD VANSPALL
P.118 PIERS BIZONY/RICHARD VANSPALL
P.119 EDWARD EFFRON
P.121 PIERS BIZONY/RICHARD VANSPALL
P.122 PIERS BIZONY/RICHARD VANSPALL
P.123 TIM STREET-PORTER/EWA
P.124 MICHAEL DUNNE/EWA
P.125 PIERS BIZONY/RICHARD VANSPALL
P.126 PIERS BIZONY/RICHARD VANSPALL
P.127 EWA
P.129 PIERS BIZONY/RICHARD VANSPALL
P.130 PIERS BIZONY/RICHARD VANSPALL
P.131 PIERS BIZONY/RICHARD VANSPALL
P.132 JON BOUCHIER/EWA
P.133 MICHAEL DUNNE/EWA
P.134 PIERS BIZONY/RICHARD VANSPALL
P.135 MICHAEL DUNNE/EWA
P.138 ANDREA VON EINSIEDEL/EWA
P.139 ANN KELLEY/EWA
P.140 EWA
P.141 ANN KELLEY/EWA
P.142 KARL-DIETRICH BUHLER/EWA
P.143 JUDITH ROBERTSON
P.144 JUDITH ROBERTSON
P.146/7 KARL-DIETRICH BUHLER/EWA
P.147 ACTIVITY SPORTS AND TOYS
P.148 PETER WOLOSZYNSKI/EWA
P.149 JUDITH ROBERTSON
P.150 EWA
P.151 KARL-DIETRICH BUHLER/EWA
P.152 JUDITH ROBERTSON
P.153 KARL-DIETRICH BUHLER-EWA
P.154 ACTIVITY SPORTS AND TOYS
P.155 KARL-DIETRICH BUHLER-EWA
P.156/7 MICHAEL DUNNE/EWA
P.159 JUDITH ROBERTSON (both)
P.169 PIERS BIZONY/RICHARD VANSPALL
P.171 DI LEWIS/EWA